SECRETS OF SPIRITUAL STAMINA

Shaw Books by Stuart Briscoe

Foundations of the Faith Series

The Apostles' Creed: Beliefs That Matter

The Fruit of the Spirit: Cultivating Christian Character

The Ten Commandments: Playing by the Rules

Understanding the Book Series

1 Peter: Holy Living in a Hostile World

Philippians: Happiness beyond Our Happenings

Titus: Living As God's Very Own People

Secrets of Spiritual Stamina

Stuart Briscoe

Harold Shaw Publishers
Wheaton, Illinois

ISBN 0-87788-757-8

Library of Congress Cataloging-in-Publication Data

Briscoe, D. Stuart.
Secrets of spiritual stamina : healthy habits for a lasting faith / Stuart Briscoe.
p. cm.
ISBN 0-87788-757-8
1. Christian life—1960- 2. Bible. N.T. Colossians—Study and teaching.
I. Title.
BV4501.2.B742 1994
248.4—dc20 94-2438
CIP

---

99 98 97 96 95 94

10 9 8 7 6 5 4 3 2 1

Contents

Where Am I Heading?

How Should I Act?

Who Can I Count On?

How Does My Family Fit In?

What about Work?

How Can I Get Involved?

How Can I Stay on Track?

Introduction

The advertiser knew his craft. Early morning light streamed through the windows of a health club. Varied patterns of light danced on gleaming weights and rowing machines and Nautilus equipment and various other instruments of self-inflicted torture.

Into this scene walked a man in street clothes. He began to talk of all the benefits of working out and getting in good shape. And then, to my surprise, he held up a copy of the *New York Times*.

"Some of you may not be able to lift this," he said, pointing to the weights, "but you can lift this"—holding up the newspaper.

His point was simple and well taken. Many folks are interested in growing physically, in bulking up, in working out. That's great! But what about working out mentally? Who wants to be big in brawn but bare in brain? People need to do something to develop their intellectual grasp of the world around them.

Notice the line the salesman took. Starting with what people were interested in, he worked to something they were less interested in. He led them from a greater interest—physical wellness—to a lesser one—intellectual wellness.

Let me borrow from that advertisement. Some of you are lifting weights, jogging, dieting. You are vitally interested in conditioning your bodies and being physically fit. God bless you, so you should! I would encourage you to lift weights, and to lift the newspaper as well, to keep in touch with your body and in tune with your world.

But I want to go a step further. You need also to be lifting your Bibles.

If you really want to get in shape, make sure you're growing not only physically and intellectually, but also spiritually.

That's what this book is all about. It's written for those who want to begin "spiritual weight training."

Have you just begun on the Christian journey, unsure about what to do next? Then join me for some biblical workouts.

Or have you been a believer for a long time, become dissatisfied with your spiritual conditioning, and decided it's time to get into shape? You are welcome as well.

We'll focus on highlights from Paul's epistle to the Colossians, a powerful little book for "people on the grow." We'll select a few key passages, arrange them by theme, and go from there.

Colossians is an ideal book for those who want to begin getting into shape spiritually. It contains one of the most solid, profound, condensed statements concerning the Lord Jesus Christ to be found anywhere in Scripture. Paul lays a solid theology in the book's first two chapters, then carefully applies that theology in the last two chapters.

Whenever you look into Scripture, you'll find things to believe and corresponding ways to behave. For Christians, believing and behaving go hand in hand.

Some people want to believe in such a way that it doesn't affect their behavior. They like you to keep it theological, theoretical; they don't want it getting practical. That way they can keep their religion locked up for a convenient hour or so on a Sunday morning without having it intrude into the rest of their week.

Others say, "Don't bother me with theology; just give me something to help. I've had a terrible week. I've had to create; I've had to work; I've really been putting out all week. Don't make me think! I mean, religion is supposed to let you switch off your mind. Just give me something practical."

Paul says, "No! I'm not interested in quick fixes that won't last. I want you to understand that underlying the practical solutions to problems are profound theological principles."

This is one of the things that makes Paul so tremendously helpful. He gives us a theological base and on that base builds a practical application. He gives theological insight, then shows how that truth works out practically in everyday life.

He follows that pattern throughout Colossians. First he states a certain truth. Then he applies that truth, and finally he requires some action of obedience based on that application. Truth is stated, then is applied, then is to be obeyed.

That's the method we'll follow in this book. We'll see what God wants to teach us, ascertain how it is to be applied to our own lives, and determine to obey what we've been shown.

That's the only way to real growth—physical, intellectual, or spiritual. By God's grace, let's determine to do it.

And let's begin today!

Who Is Jesus?

The prize lay on the table. A new computer! Excitedly its owner cut open the box. Gingerly he took the machine out, studied its manual, and connected all the appropriate wires. Eagerly he flipped on the power switch.

Nothing.

Puzzled, the man switched the computer to "Off" and rechecked all connections. He rounded up a screwdriver and fastened the wires more securely. He reread the relevant portion of the manual. Satisfied that he'd followed directions, once more he flipped the computer on.

Nothing.

Confusion turned to anger. What had those salespeople stuck him with? Didn't they say it had been "100 percent tested"?

He was mad. His dealer would hear about this! He reached for the telephone to demand his money back. Just then his little daughter walked into the room.

"Hi, Daddy!" her cheery voice rang out. "What a pretty computer! Can I plug it in?"

In the excitement of having a new toy, the man missed the one thing he couldn't afford to forget.

How often that happens to us in our Christian lives! We concentrate on the details of life and neglect Christ. We focus on all kinds of human systems and lose sight of Christ. We listen to all sorts of human authorities and forget that all authority resides in Christ. We get off into the latest ideas and kicks and therapies and somehow forget that only in Christ do we find reality.

Paul was constantly warning people on that point. He returned to it again and again and insists that we return there, too.

The whole of the first two chapters of Colossians rings with the truth that all reality is found in Christ. All the fullness of the Godhead dwells in him! He is head over all things! In Christ is to be found all authority!

If anyone ever comes near to confuse you with theories, ideas, approaches, and emphases that draw your attention away from Christ, you know that's a person to avoid. Always we must turn our eyes upon Jesus.

That is the word for the church today. Learn Christ! Focus on him! Meditate on what he has done!

Forget him, and you're in peril. Remember and honor him, and you will find your life revolutionized.

Isn't that, after all, why he came?

In God's Image

He is the image of the invisible God. Colossians 1:15

When Paul says that Christ is "the image of the invisible God," he means that Christ came to give us a visible expression of a God who is invisible. "He who has seen me has seen the Father," Jesus told his disciples. That is why no one with access to a Bible can claim ignorance of what God is like.

But he is much more than that. Jesus Christ is a reflection to us of what man was intended to be.

One of the remarkable, enigmatic things about man is his schizophrenia. Creativity oozes from his pores. He can do such magnificent things. Walk around the world with half an eye open, and you'll be awestruck at the sheer brilliance of mankind.

At the same time, however, we humans are capable of inexplicable cruelty and hostility. We pervert and pollute the most precious and beautiful things in the most dastardly, cowardly way imaginable.

How can these two impulses co-exist? How can mankind be so creative and yet so destructive? I submit that the only adequate theory sees mankind as having a marred vestige of the divine image. We were created perfect, but we fell. Then Christ came into the world, and against a fallen humanity, he stands supreme. In so doing he demonstrates how far we have fallen.

If ever we want to know how we're doing as human beings, we mustn't compare ourselves with ourselves. Instead we must measure ourselves against Jesus, the image of the invisible God—the sort of person man was intended to be in the first place.

That leads to something else. Scripture teaches that the Lord Jesus came into the world, died and rose again, then sent his Spirit into the hearts of the redeemed. The objective of the indwelling Spirit, Scripture clearly says, is to work in the hearts of reborn men and women so that ultimately they will be restored to the image of God.

This process will come to its glorious consummation when we stand before the Lord. When we see Jesus, Scripture says we will be like him. What will that mean? Since he is the image of the invisible God, when we see him we will be like him—the image of the invisible God. We will be restored to our full humanity. Christ, through his Spirit, is changing us more and more into his image.

What is one of the areas God is working on in your life to help you be more like Christ?

Thank you, Father, for sending Christ into the world to show us what you are like, and how we ought to be. Please help me to be more like him in the area of:

Firstborn, Not Created

He is . . . the firstborn over all creation. Colossians 1:15

This expression has been embraced with great delight by many cultists who deny the deity of the Lord Jesus. Many of you have been visited by Jehovah's Witnesses. Probably you have listened for a long time while they deliver their spiel. I have no doubt they have quoted this verse to you, and in quoting it have said, "There you are! That proves that he is created, which shows quite conclusively he could not possibly be equal with God."

The remarkable thing about these people is the size of their blinders. For verse 16 immediately goes on to say, "By him all things were created." And verse 17 adds, "He is before all things." And the next verse concludes everything by saying, "In everything he might have the supremacy."

This verse does not mean that Jesus Christ was the first thing created. That would be to misunderstand what "firstborn" meant in Jewish culture.

The firstborn in a Jewish family was heir in a very special way, with special privileges and responsibilities.

When Paul says Christ is God's firstborn, he means that Jesus rightfully inherits from the Father absolutely everything that was created. *Everything*. Nothing is excluded; nothing is left out. Jesus is "His Majesty" in the ultimate, true, and full sense!

I once heard Jack Hayford tell how a tour of Britain prompted him to write the popular song "Majesty." He saw the crown jewels, Buckingham Palace, the guards. He witnessed all the panoply, the majesty, the glory, the magnificence of royalty, and was moved to sit down while still in Britain and write his song.

Sometimes the culture we live in undermines our sense of majesty—even the majesty of our Lord Jesus Christ. How unfortunate that is! For Christ is the very epitome, the zenith, of what "majesty" is about. Majestic, exalted, lofty, regal, stately, grand—he is all that and more!

Most of us will never meet a ruling monarch. But we will meet the King one day—and every day should be lived in the consciousness of that event.

What events in the life of Christ, or what aspects of his character, give you a sense of his majesty?

Father, please give me a new realization of the majesty of your Son.

In the Beginning

For by him all things were created: things in heaven and on earth, visible and invisible, whether thrones or powers or rulers or authorities; all things were created by him and for him. He is before all things.
Colossians 1:16-17

The president of the United States of America wields awesome power as the commander-in-chief of all U.S. military forces. Even he, however, can't do just what he likes with that power. The sphere of his operation is the constitution. When he takes his oath as president, he pledges to operate within the confines of the constitution.

In the same way, God the Father has chosen to use all his mighty power in creation exclusively in and through Christ. Absolutely everything that was created—in heaven or on earth; visible or invisible; thrones, powers, rulers, authorities—was created through him and for him.

That assumes that Jesus existed before anything was created. And that's exactly what Paul means. Far from being part of creation, and far from creation being part of him, Jesus is before all things. John says the same thing in John 1:1—"In the beginning was the Word, and the Word was with God, and the Word was God." Before anything was made, John says, the Word was continually in existence.

While that's a powerful statement, it's also hard to get a handle on.

We can get a handle on the Incarnation. We love little babies in mangers. We love the idea of everyone bowing down and worshiping before the manger. We can get a handle on Jesus the man, that Christ was beaten, maltreated, betrayed, deserted, cruelly scourged, and viciously crucified.

We can even get excited about the idea of Jesus' rising from the dead in a resurrection body and appearing to his disciples.

The thing we have a hard time handling is that this incarnate, rejected, crucified, maligned, spat-upon Jesus existed before anything was created.

Unless we do begin to think of him in those terms, however, the significance of his incarnation, death, and resurrection will elude us. It was the pre-existent one who laid aside his glory, assumed our humanity, and stepped down into our life.

When it says he is before all things, it doesn't say "before all things were created, he *was*." That would be good grammar but bad theology. Jesus does not operate on the basis of tenses as we do. We think in terms of past and present and future, but Jesus has only one tense—the present. Before all things were created, he *is*. He is the pre-existent, eternal one.

That explains his superior status. Nothing created can possibly rank ahead of him. This is why idolatry is so detestable, for idolaters value the created thing more highly than the Creator. Idolatry is elevating created things above the one by, in, through, and for whom all things were created.

Do I now value any created thing more than I value Jesus Christ? Practically speaking, is there anything or anyone that is presently more important to me than he is?

Lord Jesus, today I acknowledge that I was made through, by, and for you. Please help me to live that out today in everything I do.

He's in Charge

In him all things hold together. Colossians 1:17

Sometimes when I'm preaching I get all worked up. And on occasion when I've gotten all worked up I have banged my hand on our solid oak pulpit. I assure you it is solid, and that its edges are very sharp.

Occasionally I rap my knuckles on one of those sharp edges, and immediately thereafter my congregation thinks, *Wow, is he preaching up a storm!* No, I am not. I'm in agony. There is nothing quite so solid as a solid oak pulpit, particularly when you rap your knuckles on it and you are only halfway through your second point. In other words, another forty minutes to go in torment.

I do take some comfort in discovering that solid matter is not really solid at all. It's really made up of space, with a few little things whizzing around inside it. I confess I don't understand it. But I understand on good authority that everything we regard as solid is in fact made up of infinitesimally small objects, called atoms, held together by space. And the space is held together by some indescribable, indefinable power.

Now, of course, some very smart people discovered the atom. And they said that's what we are made up of. But then some very, very smart people said, "Aha! The atom is made up of all sorts of smaller things." In fact, you can split an atom and discover protons, neutrons, croutons, what have you, and all these things are held together by some strange, powerful force.

All the time they are probing further and further. What they're discovering is less and less, bound together by the most phenomenal power. And nobody on earth knows what it is.

All things, in some strange way, hold together. To the best of my knowledge, there is absolutely no reason why you and I, being made mostly of space, should not just disintegrate. What a mess that would be.

But all our universe is held together, and scientific minds all over the planet are seeking to understand why. Physicists and mathematicians are puzzling over it. They're all trying to figure it out.

Could it be that the clue is found, of all places, in the Bible? It says that "in him all things hold together."

Do you begin to get a glimmer of the mind-boggling dimensions of King Jesus?

What are some examples in your life of things that are held together by Christ?

Thank you, Father, that in Jesus Christ the universe and our lives are held together.

Are You Coordinated?

And he is the head of the body, the church. Colossians 1:18

Some time ago I went down to Brazil with Jill for some meeting. While there I made inquiries about seeing a soccer match. An Englishman just grieves over not being able to see soccer when he's living in a foreign land, but if you can go to Brazil, that's the next best thing. They told me there was only one game in the whole of Brazil that weekend, and it was the equivalent of our Super Bowl game.

"Is there the remotest chance that we can get tickets? Could you please get me a ticket to see that game?"

"What a relief!" they exclaimed. "We'd all gotten tickets, and we didn't think we could go because you'd want to have a meeting."

"Oh, no, no! Jill can do the meeting," I explained. "We'll go to the game."

Our excitement grew when we entered the vast stadium and began to feel the thrill of the Super Bowl of Brazilian soccer. We took our seats, and the game began. The teams were evenly matched; neither could get an advantage over the other. Near the end of the game there was still no score.

Suddenly the right winger cut away, beat his man, crossed the ball, and our man came right down the middle with a phenomenal burst of speed. He gauged his run until his head intersected with the ball, a fabulous piece of judgment. He came between two defenders, headed up the ball, brought it down on his chest, held his arms out to keep from touching it, and with his chest brought the ball down onto his left knee. He flipped it up onto his right foot, took it around a man, and hit it on the half volley with his left foot. It went straight into the top corner of the net. That made the score 1-0 and won the game.

Why do I explain all that to you? Because it demonstrates just how wonderfully coordinated the human body is.

Now, the church is described in many different ways, but perhaps the model we are most familiar with is the idea of it as a body. We all know what a body does and how it functions. In this passage, Paul says that Jesus Christ controls and coordinates members of the fellowship and holds the church together as a head controls a body.

Christ is the head of the body, the church, and the church can be a disaster or it can be phenomenal. The key to making it phenomenal is to allow the Lord Jesus to be the controlling factor of each member. Individual members must allow Jesus' Spirit to direct them to be what he wants them to be and to do what he wants them to do. There can be none of this individual stuff, but instead a tremendous sense of his overarching control and wise coordination.

What can each person do to help the church, as one body, to be truly under Christ's control?

Lord, please help me as I struggle to submit to your coordination in these areas:

The Supreme Commander

He is the beginning and the firstborn from among the dead, so that in everything he might have the supremacy. Colossians 1:18

Here is the idea of firstborn again. It does not mean he was the first to rise from the dead. We know that isn't true. He raised some from the dead himself. But he was the firstborn from the dead in the sense that when he arose from the dead, he could never die again.

In being the firstborn, he was heir to eternal life. As heir, he can dispense it to all. He, in his resurrection, made it possible for us to be raised into newness of life.

When we are raised into newness of life by the risen Christ, that's a new beginning. We're alive in the power of his resurrection. He becomes the dynamic of our life.

So what's the church? The church is a group of people indwelt by the life of the risen Christ, raised in newness of life in him, controlled by him as head, coordinated into a cohesive body in which his Spirit moves in his ancient ways.

Now the church, unfortunately, sometimes gets a long way away from Jesus. As soon as it does, it becomes not the body, but the corpse.

The thing that makes the church is not the preacher, nor the elders, nor its people. The thing that makes the church the church is the head, Christ, who is powerfully at work in individual lives. The church is utterly dependent upon him.

And then Paul sort of grabs the whole thing together and says, "So in everything he is supreme."

Do you remember Operation Overload—the Normandy invasion of World War II? Until that time the armies of the

Allies served under various commanders. But now they came together to attack the stronghold of Nazi Germany. It was necessary that there be a supreme commander. You couldn't have the British commanded by the British any longer, and the Americans by an American, and the Australians by an Australian. Free French, Belgians, Norwegians—you couldn't have them all doing their own thing. There had to be a supreme commander, and Dwight Eisenhower was that man.

He did a wonderful job. But with all due respect to Mr. Eisenhower, he was not *the* Supreme Commander. That title is reserved for the one who is King of kings and Lord of lords, that in everything he might have the supremacy.

If we are to enjoy life in the kingdom, it is in relationship to the King. And if our relationship to the King is to be right, our understanding of him must be constantly enlarged.

You never need worry about enlarging overmuch in your understanding of the Lord Jesus. Learn as much as you can, as long as you can. After eighty years, you'll still be skin and bones in proportion to the amount there is to devour.

Just think of it—mounds and mounds of luscious, delectable truth about King Jesus, inviting you to sit down and indulge. Enlarge yourself in your knowledge of Christ the King! It's the one area where dieting is downright harmful to your health!

Why is it important for us to constantly learn more about our Supreme Commander?

Father, please help me to know what my Supreme Commander wants me to do today, and help me to do it in your strength.

All I Need

For God was pleased to have all his fullness dwell in him.
Colossians 1:19

Have you ever come to know and admire someone of great gifts and ability, only to discover later you didn't know the half of it?

Something like that apparently happened late in 1987 to film critics across the country. Many thought of director Steven Spielberg as a one-dimensional talent, a fellow who put out cute, wholesome fantasies (like *E.T.*). His pictures may not mean much, the critics said, but they're great fun.

Then Spielberg released a film titled *Empire of the Sun*. It told the story of a young English boy interned by the Japanese from 1941 to 1945 in occupied China. The critics were astonished—Spielberg wasn't thought capable of creating a thoughtful picture like *Empire*.

If you take that astonishment and multiply it by a billion, you will get a glimmer of the awe and amazement that Jesus prompted in the apostle Paul.

Paul knew that Jesus is magnificent in the creation. He knew that Jesus is magnificent in the church. But he also knew that Jesus is magnificent in the Christian. His greatness is magnified in what he does in the lives and hearts of the redeemed.

When Jesus came to earth as the God-Man, "God was pleased to have all his fullness dwell in him." Everything that makes God was present in Christ.

That had special significance for the church at Colosse. When Paul wrote his letter, the church was battling some heretics who quite probably were teaching a doctrine that eventually would develop into something called Gnosticism. This heresy nearly demolished the church of the second century.

Gnostics stressed two ideas. First, they taught that to really understand spiritual things you had to be initiated in a special way—their way. "We have all the truth," they said. "Do it our way or forget it." If you had not gained this special enlightenment, this special knowledge, you hadn't even gotten to square one.

Second, they believed that matter was evil and spirit was good. Therefore God, who is Spirit, could have nothing to do with the creation, which was material and evil. Spirit and matter could never touch.

Paul came around and said, "No, matter is not evil; all things were created by Christ and through him and for him. In Christ you have everything you need for true spiritual experience."

That is profound. We need to be reminded that God was pleased to have all his fullness dwell in Christ, and that all his fullness is available to us.

What are some of the aspects of the "fullness of God," found in Christ, that we need to be more aware of and apply to our lives every day?

Father, thank you that all I need of you is available in Christ. Please help me to come closer to you through him and learn to fully appreciate all you have given to me.

Putting Things Together Again

For God was pleased . . . through him to reconcile to himself all things, whether things on earth or things in heaven, by making peace through his blood, shed on the cross. Colossians 1:19-20

Paul says that this one, in whom dwells everything needed for spiritual satisfaction, is the one through whom God sought to reconcile all things to himself.

When Paul says God will reconcile to himself all things, he doesn't say God is going to reconcile all *people*. He doesn't say everyone will end up in heaven. To believe that is to deny Scripture. Salvation is available to all. But not all will respond. He does not reconcile all people to himself. He reconciles in Christ all things to himself.

What does that mean?

Let's back up a little. When man fell, society began to disintegrate. When society began to disintegrate, ecology got out of whack. When ecology got out whack, all kinds of things went wrong. As a result, we have loads of tension, disease, hurt, and heartache. In short, when mankind fell, everything came unglued.

That will all change when God puts things back together in a new heaven and a new earth, where Christ will be King of kings and Lord of lords. At that time he will reconcile all things to himself. And then everything will be the opposite of out of whack. What's that? In whack. All things will be in whack.

And all this is possible because Christ made peace through his blood, shed on the cross. Having given us a glorious vista of the magnificence of the Lord Jesus, Paul says we appreciate it only to the degree that we see this pre-existent one laying aside his glory, assuming our humanity, dying our death, giving his life, and shedding his blood so we can be forgiven and reconciled to God. That's quite a resume!

Do you appreciate who Jesus is and what he has done for you? I'm not asking if you have accepted Christ as your Savior. I hope that you have, and that if you haven't, you will. What I'm wondering about is the depth of your affection for Jesus himself, as your Friend, Brother, Savior, God, and Lord.

Have you told him recently what he means to you? Have you thought about his willing sacrifice on your behalf? Have you thanked him for his care of you? Do you brag about him to others?

Take some time, right now, to treasure this Jesus. Take a moment to talk to him. Not because you have to, or because guilt makes you, but because he is worthy! Jesus is magnificent in the Christian—that's you, and that's me.

Let's thank him for it!

How does God "reconcile to himself all things"?

Father, thank you for paying such a great price to bring us to yourself. And thank you for your work in my life.

The Mystery Solved

My purpose is . . . that they may know the mystery of God, namely, Christ. Colossians 2:2

There's something tantalizing about a secret.

Secrets have an almost irresistible power to arouse our curiosity, to whet our thirst for a bit of information no one else has.

Do you remember how as a child, one of the most irritating taunts anyone could flip your way was—in that awful sing-song voice—"I know something you don't know!"

Many cults use the lure of secrets to charm the unwary into their web of lies. "We know the hidden way to God," they whisper. "Join us and learn the secret. Nobody else can help you. Nobody else knows what it is. We alone have the answer. Come on inside. We can't talk out here."

Something just like that was going on in Paul's time. In those days "mystery religions" were sprouting up all over. People outside their cliques hadn't a clue what went on inside. People on the inside believed they understood the secrets of the universe; its mysteries were no mystery to them.

Paul borrows that little word *mystery* here and uses it for his own purposes. When he writes about a mystery, he's not talking about an Agatha Christie–style mystery, where God is sitting up there spinning a tale intended to confuse. What he's saying is, "Look, do you really want to understand how the universe is put together? Do you really want to know the mystery of God? Then come to Christ. Christ is the mystery of God; Christ is the one who unveils God. Commit yourself to Christ, and you'll begin to understand what you never understood before—who God really is."

Is that something you'd like? Would getting a clearer vision of God meet a desperate need in your life? If so, you need to know Christ more fully.

You needn't join some secretive, select clique huddled off in some corner to do so. You don't need some secret initiation rite or a specially trained tutor to learn about Jesus. The Christ you need to know was crucified publicly, was resurrected in power and written about in the Gospels, and is available to anyone who calls upon him. The mystery of God has been openly revealed in Jesus. Paul said as much in Colossians 1:28: "We proclaim him, admonishing and teaching everyone with all wisdom, so that we may present everyone perfect in Christ."

Why do you think Christ is described here as "the mystery of God"?

Heavenly Father, thank you for the beauty and the simplicity of the fact that all your mystery is summed up in Christ. Please help me to come to know him better, and thus to know you better.

Hidden Treasures

Christ, in whom are hidden all the treasures of wisdom and knowledge.
Colossians 2:2-3

This Christ, who is the mystery of God, is the one in whom are hidden all the treasures of wisdom and knowledge. What a prize for people searching out truth!

Have you noticed that this search goes on all the time? We're constantly encouraged to look into all areas of knowledge. There's an explosion of it. The minute you write an encyclopedia, it's out of date. The folks over at the *Encyclopedia Britannica* think it's great. If ever you get on their enrollment, you'll get books coming every few minutes. You'll never have time to read them, but they keep coming.

When we look into all these areas of knowledge, it's easy to become confused. It's possible to get sidetracked.

Some people say, "Wow, look at all this stuff! I'm going to get off into these areas," and they forget Christ.

Others recognize that danger and say, "Well, I won't study anything, then. I'll just study Christ."

There's a balance we've got to maintain. All truth is God's truth, but what determines whether it's true is its agreement with Christ.

As I study psychology, philosophy, cosmology, futurology, I test everything by Christ to see whether it's skewed: If what I'm discovering in philosophy is flatly contradictory to Christ, then that philosophy is wrong. If what I'm studying in psychology contravenes what Christ taught, then I put that psychology on the side of the plate.

The bottom line is this: If all the treasures of wisdom and knowledge are found in Christ, then anything that opposes Christ is wrong.

Christ is the one from whom all things emanate. He is the one by, for, and through whom all things were created. He is the one who ultimately will rule and reign when everything is made subject to him.

Because this is true, we've got to encourage each other to know him. In knowing him we'll have the mystery of God opened up to us—not to keep to ourselves as some closely guarded secret, but as a treasure to enrich those around us.

And here's the kicker: You can tell this secret without spoiling the fun, and share this treasure without making it shrink.

You won't find that kind of bounty anywhere else in the universe.

What is one area of your knowledge that you'd like to examine in light of your knowledge of Christ?

Father, I want all my knowledge to fit into your scheme of things. Please give me the wisdom, through Christ, to discern what is true and worth studying.

Down to Earth

For in Christ all the fullness of the Deity lives in bodily form.
Colossians 2:9

This verse ought to be so heavily underlined in your Bible that it comes right through to the leather binding. It is so important. If you forget that in Christ is found all the fullness of deity in bodily form, you will have a shallow view of his reality. If you have a shallow view of the reality of Christ, your relationship with him will suffer—and the essence of your life is relationship with Christ.

All that goes to make God *God* is invested in the Lord Jesus Christ. If there is anything you want to know about God, look to Christ. If it is truth, life, or righteousness you are interested in, look to Christ. All those things emanate from the very being, nature, and essence of God and are found in Christ.

But that's not where people today look for them. When men and women search for truth, life, and righteousness today, where do they look? All over the place. Even believers!

Paul brings us back to square one and says, "No, all that makes God what he is, all that is good, right, true, and real, is demonstrated in Christ. Don't wander from him in your search for reality."

Notice Paul's emphasis on God's fullness (which is spiritual) residing in Christ's body (which is physical).

Remember the Gnostic heresy, which taught that spiritual is good and physical is bad, and that the two could never mix any more than good and evil could mix? But Paul insists that God's Spirit is found in Christ, as man, in bodily form.

This emphasis on the physical reminds us of the Incarnation, the Crucifixion, the Resurrection, and the Ascension.

In the Incarnation, this wonderful God came to be with us.

In the Crucifixion, this wonderful God chose to die for us.

In the Resurrection, this wonderful God gave us life.

In the Ascension, this wonderful God gave us hope and access to the Father.

When we think of all the fullness in bodily form, we rejoice that this wonderful God—in whom truth and righteousness and reality and life are to be found—lived among us, died for us, and now constantly prays for us.

This is the basis of our faith. Never let yourself be diverted from it!

Be warned that deceivers will try to deflect your attention from Christ. They will pervert the gospel and oppose the lordship of Christ.

Beware! Remember that all reality is found in Christ. Remember that this Christ is the one with whom we have a living relationship.

How does Colossians 2:9 refute the Gnostic heresy?

Thank you, Father, that by coming to us in Christ you not only showed us how to live out truth and righteousness, but you came to be with us, die for us, and give us life, hope, and access to yourself.

Alive and Available

For in Christ all the fullness of the Deity lives in bodily form.
Colossians 2:9

It has often been said that Christianity is not so much a religion as a relationship. This is easy to say and, accordingly, is often misunderstood. The point of it is this: The major religions of the world are attempts by man to follow the teachings of dead prophets. Christianity, on the other hand, is the incredible privilege of a redeemed man or woman living in relationship with a risen, living, exalted Lord.

The essence of Christianity is not found in trying to follow the teachings of a dead Jesus. The essence of Christianity is that you and I can be related to God through Jesus, the divine Son of God, who was incarnate, was crucified, is risen, and lives in the power of an endless life.

That is why the rest of Colossians 2:9-13 is riddled with the expressions "in him" and "with him." It is in Christ (in relationship to him) and with him (in relationship with him) that genuine spiritual experience is to be found.

It's possible to find all kinds of spiritual experiences outside of Christ. People do it all the time. But if you want the real thing, the thing that satisfies, fulfills, strengthens, completes, comforts, and delights, you'll never find it until you search for it, grasp it, and rest in it in Christ.

"In Christ all the fullness of the Deity lives in bodily form." All the boundless power and strength that "fullness" implies is available to every believer in Christ. Are you taking advantage of it?

How much of your time is spent striving to follow Christ's example, and how much is spent just being with him and developing your relationship?

Thank you, Father, that the Leader we follow is not dead, but very much alive and available to us.

So What?

Therefore . . . Colossians 2:16

It's quite possible for a writer to have a marvelous time spouting out theology by the mile, while those out in the workaday world are trying to pay debts, raise kids, handle bosses, and deal with all kinds of nasty, hard, difficult relationships. So while the writer—me—is having a marvelous time with his theology, his readers sit there impatiently asking, "So what?"

Some try to get over this hump by starting with where people are and leaving it at that, never bringing Jesus into the discussion. We can't do that. The "so what" of Paul's teaching about Jesus is very simple. Let me suggest three things.

First, if Jesus Christ is head of creation and head of the church—and he is!—then we don't have the freedom to do what the Gnostics were doing. We can't say, "Well, one part of my life is sacred and the rest of it is secular. Sunday morning I'll act religious, but the rest of the week is mine. I'll keep my spiritual experience in a watertight compartment while living the vast majority of my life in the secular realm. I'll make sure the two never connect."

Jesus refuses to give us that option. He created all things. He is the head of the church. Our spiritual experience and our natural, material experience—both come from him and come under his lordship. Therefore, we are not free to talk about "the sacred" and "the secular."

Second, if Christ is supreme, he is absolutely sufficient. He created the world and keeps it going. We worship the

Creator of all things, the one who upholds everything by the word of his power. Therefore, he can work in our lives, too.

Do we believe that? Too often we think, *He can handle the universe, but not me. The universe must bow to him, but I don't need to bow myself.* What foolishness!

Fortunately, Jesus doesn't allow us to carry on like that for long. He is supreme, and he is sufficient. He is the King, and sooner or later we will be called into his presence to acknowledge the fact. How much better to do so with joy!

Third, Jesus is the unifying and unique factor of all existence. There is nothing we can add to him. Nothing. Therefore, don't try. As he is the unifying factor, we can keep nothing from him. He is the King of kings and Lord of lords, and everything we have—everything—belongs ultimately to him.

Charles Wesley was certainly right. Pondering that first Christmas morning, he wrote of the infant Jesus, "God contracted to a span, incomprehensibly made man." Only when we accept this and revel in it do we begin to see the significance of the magnificence of King Jesus. And only then do we begin to really live! "Therefore . . ."

Hail, King Jesus!

What is your response to what you have studied in Colossians so far? What is your "Therefore . . ."?

Father, thank you so much for what you teach us in your Word, and for how it changes us. I pray that what I have learned so far would change me in these ways:

Meditations on Christ

1. Read Philippians 2:5-11 and think about which aspects of Christ's experience we can imitate and which belong to him alone.

2. Take some time to meditate on Hebrews 1:1–3:6. Try reading it out loud a few times.

3. Memorize Hebrews 12:2-3.

4. What does 1 Peter 2:18-25 say about how Christ handled unjust treatment? What are some clues we find in the passage about the key to handling it the way he did?

5. Have someone read the fifth chapter of Revelation aloud to you. Close your eyes and try to imagine what John saw in his vision.

What's a Christian?

There are some clubs I've never been in, and there are many, many clubs of which I'm not a part. But I really don't care, because I qualify for the greatest club in the world. Let me tell you about my membership.

I am a member of the Saints in Light, and I have available to me all the inheritance of God. And I qualify, not because of anything I did, but because Jesus took me by the hand, introduced me, and recommended me for membership. Boy, am I thankful!

My life has changed because God touched my life and gave me the light of the knowledge of himself, casting out the darkness, ignorance, shame, and sin, washing it all away, and setting me apart for himself.

I'm thankful for emancipation, too. You see, Christ rescued me from the dominion of darkness. Spiritual ignorance, disgrace, and guilt no longer reign in my life.

Through Christ's death and resurrection I was delivered from ignorance and evil, had my eyes opened to the truth, and was rescued from all things I was ashamed of. He set me free and gave me a new life.

I don't need to chase after every new thrill that comes along. I don't need to spend my time and energy looking for something else. What do they matter?

I've become a member of the kingdom of the Son of his love, and I'm thankful for the redemption I have in him. Redemption means freedom from sin's power and forgiveness of sin's record, and it was purchased for me by Jesus on the cross.

I will never forget what he did. I will never forget what it cost him. And I will never stop being grateful to him. Somebody has said that the theology of Christianity is grace and the ethic of Christianity is gratitude. I couldn't have said it better myself. When I understand what God in his grace has done for me, the spontaneous response of my heart is thankfulness.

Is it fulfillment you want? You'll only find it in a rich relationship to the living God.

Is it satisfaction you crave? You'll only find it in a life of loving devotion to God.

When you're fully involved in doing good, in trying to please God, a full life is the natural result. Do that, and you'll find yourself living a winsome, distinctively attractive Christian life.

It's called fulfillment. And it's found in a living, growing relationship with Christ.

A New Spirit, New Morals, and a New Mind

... to the holy and faithful brothers in Christ. Colossians 1:2

It would be easy to slide over the phrase "in Christ," but these words, common in this epistle and in all Paul's writings, are ones he loves to use to describe people who are related to the Lord Jesus. He means that Christ is the atmosphere they breathe, the dominating factor of their lives, the one who directs them in the way they ought to go.

He also means that when God looks at people who are "in Christ," he doesn't see them in all their failure. He sees them in all the righteousness of the Lord Jesus.

When Paul writes to people who are "in Christ," he is talking about their spiritual position and condition. But these people are also called "holy" from a moral point of view.

Just imagine what would happen if someone were to ask a young person in school, "What is your ambition?" and she were to reply, "I want to be holy." What would be the reaction? The class would crack up. People would think the kid was loony.

This is because we don't like the word *holy*. And we don't like it because we don't understand it.

The root from which we get the word *holy* is the word meaning "to cut," to separate something from the rest, to make it distinctive, other, something else. When God picks a word to describe himself, he uses the word *holy*. That means he's distinct, separate, other.

People who are "in Christ" spiritually are required to be holy and moral—to live distinctively. There are some things holy people won't get into. They're too smart. They won't get into destructive habits because they have a new set of priorities.

Holiness, however, shouldn't only be seen in negative terms. The basic idea of holiness is not negative, it's positive. If we are holy, we live attractive, winsome, definite, distinctive lives. People notice.

Finally, these people are described intellectually as "believing." It is important to note that the word here translated *faithful* can equally well be translated *believing*. *Faithful* and *full of faith* come from the same Greek word—they have only one word for both. If you are full of faith, you demonstrate it by being faithful. If you are trusting, you demonstrate it by being trustworthy. The two always work hand-in-glove.

These believers in Colosse had intellectually subscribed to the gospel, but it had more than intellectual ramifications. Morally it shaped their lifestyle, and spiritually it placed them into Christ.

Do you see yourself as living 'in Christ'? Do you see him as the atmosphere you breathe, the environment in which you live?

Father, thank you for placing me in Christ. Please help me today to live distinctively as your person, and to be faithful to you in all I do.

Wherever You Are

Paul . . . to the . . . brothers in Christ at Colosse. Colossians 1:2

This little group of people that we call the church at Colosse now regarded each other as brothers in Christ.

Many of them, no doubt, had run into real problems with their blood relatives. There'd been some real divisions when they became Christians. Some of you can sympathize with them. When you became a Christian, the members of your family didn't like it. They resisted what you would say and seemed to resent what you stand for. But God steps in, and in one sense, compensates. You can't totally compensate for the estrangement of your blood relatives, but there is some compensation in discovering in the fellowship of believers a whole new set of brothers and sisters.

You are part of a new family, a much bigger family. That's one reason people come to Christ in our society. With the breakup of marriage and the family, there are many lovely, lonely, discouraged, disconsolate people. But when they're introduced to Christ, they're introduced to a whole new community. In that new community they find a whole lot of new brothers and sisters.

This description is essentially practical. For Paul is sitting in a smelly cell, with a specific town in mind. He knows the people of that town and what they're up against, and he's interested in their becoming spiritually, morally, intellectually, and sociologically distinctive believers in Colosse.

Colosse had a great history, but it had fallen on hard times. It had been a superior city, but it now was being overshadowed by Laodicea and Hierapolis nearby, and Ephesus not many miles away. It was known for its paganism, a place overrun by idolatry.

The apostle says it's there—in that one-horse town with a chip on its shoulder, in that place riddled with idolatry and governed by paganism—it's in that environment that believers were called to live holy, distinctive, winsomely attractive lives.

How does all this apply to us? Very simply. The Spirit of God would say to you and me today, "Are you holy, faithful brothers in Christ in your community? In your towns and cities that are riddled with materialism and governed by greed, are you faithful representatives of my Son? The days of the Colossians are long past. It's your turn now. How're you doing?"

If you wrote a truthful letter of reply, what would it say?

> *Father, though sometimes I am too much a part of my surroundings to really notice, please help me to see clearly enough to know how I need to change to be different in the ways you want me to.*

Ground Zero

Once you were alienated from God and were enemies in your minds because of your evil behavior. Colossians 1:21

The Bible teaches that people were made by God for God, and that the only way we can truly live is in relationship to God. But we are born alienated from him, and there is an enormous hole in our lives without him.

These holes express themselves in different ways. Some people are blatantly antagonistic to God. Some of us shook our fists in his face, denied his existence, or lived brazenly opposed to everything he said. Others simply disregarded him as irrelevant.

Some of us can look back to lives that were inexpressibly evil. We lived as we pleased and couldn't care less who got hurt. Others' lives before Christ didn't seem so evil. "I was never like that," we might say. "I was just a normal, decent, law-abiding citizen."

The problem is that our standards of decency and law are such that it is quite possible to be a decent, law-abiding citizen, and still be considered evil in God's eyes. We need to measure our behavior not against normally accepted principles, but against what God has said in his Word.

Whether the antagonism is overt or covert, all Christians can testify that at one stage in their experience, they were alienated from God, not living to please God, and were earning his wrath.

Can you recall your own life before you met Christ? Do you remember the feeling of alienation, restlessness, and emptiness, the desperate search for satisfaction and self-fulfillment?

The old theologians had an explanation for this. They said there is a God-shaped vacuum inside each of us, and we'll only be fulfilled and satisfied when God himself steps into our lives to fill that God-shaped blank.

Christians have no problem agreeing with Paul's words. They say, "I remember when I was alienated from God. I remember when I was active in evil behavior. I am not proud of it, but I am so glad that Jesus came into my life, turned it around, and set me on a new course. I'm so glad I am no longer what I once was."

Can you make that kind of declaration? If you can, then I'd like to encourage you to continue growing in the faith you've embraced. It only gets better.

And if you can't, there's no time like the present to get started with God. Your chest is no place for a vacuum.

Who do you know who feels restless, empty, and alienated from God? How can you pray for that person?

Lord, please help me to remember that when I long for fulfillment, I am really longing for you, and that when I feel alienated from you, you can deal with whatever stands between us.

But Now . . .

But now he has reconciled you . . . Colossians 1:22

Suppose you lived years ago in a wild, sparsely populated portion of the old West. Suppose you had moved there with your family to transform the inhospitable countryside into lush, fertile farmland.

Then imagine that one day, all four of your darling, lively, lovely children fell ill with raging temperatures. You try waiting out the fever, but it only gets worse. You and your spouse frantically do everything you can to save your children—you bathe them in cool water, you try coaxing liquids down their feverish throats, you even invoke the help of "spirits." Nothing helps.

Finally night comes and you lie down with your mate to snatch a tiny bit of rest. You lean over to kiss your loved one's brow and are startled to find a fever raging there, too.

Desperate, you load your ailing family into your horse-drawn wagon and race toward the nearest town—a good forty miles away.

As morning breaks, you storm into town. You jump down off the wagon and bellow for a doctor. Soon a sleepy physician staggers out of his bedroom and makes his way toward you. You quickly escort him to your family and describe the sickness.

"Yes, yes, I've seen this illness many times before," the doctor says. "It's responsible for half the graves you see in our cemetery over there. People just kept getting sick; wasn't nothing I could do for 'em."

Your heart sinks.

"And, say—looks like you've got it now," he continues.

You mop your brow. The telltale signs are there, all right. You look at your family. Death seems to hover over the wagon. *How can it end like this?* your spirit screams.

"I never could do nothin' for our people when they got sick like this," you hear the doctor sigh. "So many died."

He shakes his head and quietly rustles the contents of his black bag. You hardly notice that he takes out a syringe loaded with clear liquid.

"But now . . . " he says.

What? your mind shouts. You snap out of your daze, barely catching the doctor's next words, which sound like "But now, with this new drug here, we can save all of 'em. Let's hurry and get their sleeves rolled up. This'll make 'em better in no time."

But now—the two sweetest words in your universe at that moment. Death was inches away. *But now . . .*

That's exactly the mood Paul sets in this passage. He has just told the Colossians that they were diseased, ill, as good as dead in their old life before Christ. Then he comes to verse 22: "But now he has reconciled you."

What is the significance of having the "medicine" readily available to cure the "disease" of separation from God?

Father, thank you so much for providing the remedy for our alienation from you.

By His Grace

Now he has reconciled you by Christ's physical body through death.
Colossians 1:22

Some of us believe we decided one day "to accept Jesus as our Savior." If by that we mean that one day we committed our lives to Christ, great! But we must not let that terminology move us away from a profound spiritual truth: Our salvation does not originate with us. Our salvation originates with God. It is God who has reconciled us to himself.

If we fail to see this we will never understand the grace of God. It was the grace of God that determined that we should be reconciled, determined how we should be reconciled, and made the means of reconciliation available to us. It was divine initiative from start to finish.

The only reason we can be reconciled to God, have our alienation taken away, our antagonism abolished, and our evil activities forgiven, is that God, in Christ, came into the world in the Incarnation, assumed our humanity, lived physically among us, and died a physical, horrible death on a cruel cross.

It was necessary to remind the Colossians of this, because a heresy then current suggested that experience unrelated to the physical death of Christ could lead to fullness of life.

Even today people will try to pry your attention away from Calvary to focus it on any number of self-improvement schemes. Even in the church there is a tremendous emphasis on personal fulfillment. You'll find scores of people trying to get their lives "integrated," "put together," or "reconciled."

Many of these programs so heavily emphasize individual fulfillment that they overlook the death of Christ. We need to remind ourselves that "there is salvation in no other; there is no other name under heaven given to men whereby we must be saved." We dare not move into any type of "reconciliation ministry" that ignores the death of Christ. It becomes sub-Christian the moment it does.

The only basis upon which sinful man can be reconciled to God is through the death of Christ. The wages of sin is death. We must pay it ourselves, or allow Christ to pay it for us. His death substitutes for ours. Only through his death on the cross is it possible for us to escape eternal death and everlasting separation from God.

You'll never get right with God by doing an end-run around the cross. You'll never have sins forgiven on any other basis than the death of Christ.

What happens when we start to focus on all the things we have to do to be reconciled to God?

Father, thank you so much that you have done all that is necessary in order for me to be made right with you.

Back Where I Belong

. . . to present you holy in his sight, without blemish and free from accusation. Colossians 1:22

Paul has in mind a law court in which someone is presented before the judge. The judge hears the evidence, passes sentence, pays the sentence himself, and declares the prisoner free to go. No further charges can be brought against him.

When people are reconciled to God, God brings them into his presence and declares them utterly and totally forgiven. No further charges can be brought.

Suppose someone living in a nice, quiet neighborhood commits a horrible crime. The perpetrator is brought into court and found guilty. He's packed off to jail, and twenty years later he's released and goes back to his neighborhood. You'd think that after twenty years the people would have forgotten, wouldn't you? You'd think that after twenty years in jail people would say, "Boy, he's paid his dues. Let's receive the guy back again." But that doesn't happen very often. Often he discovers he's not very welcome in the neighborhood. Guilt is still attached to him.

I've got great news for you. When you are justified by God, you're welcome back in God's neighborhood. He doesn't keep hitting you over the head with what you did. He doesn't keep laying a guilt trip on you. You are justified. You are presented before him holy, without blemish, free from accusation.

A Christian can look back and say, "That's what I was, but this is what I am. I am reconciled. I have been justified. No guilt attached."

What are some of the things in your life, forgiven by God, that you still feel guilty about? How can you be free from accusation, even from yourself?

Father, thank you for making me pure and holy in your sight, and for not remembering my failures. Now please help me to let the past go as well.

Don't Run on Empty

You have been given fullness in Christ. Colossians 2:10

Imagine that you have been invited to Thanksgiving dinner at the home of the richest man in the world. You pull up a chair at a table two football fields long that's piled high with so much turkey, dressing, potatoes, bread, carrot cake, pumpkin pie, mixed vegetables, milk, and anything else you can think of that the table is about to break under the load. Your host tells you to take your fill of anything you see.

"Thank you very much," you say. "Might I please have half a cranberry?"

Your astonished friend nearly chokes on a candied yam and replies, "Please have all you would like. That's why I invited you! You're hungry, and here is everything you need to get full."

"Thank you so very much," you say. "Perhaps I will have a sip of water."

Ridiculous, we say. Who would ever act like that? If it were us, we'd gobble up so much food they'd have to use a bulldozer to move us out.

Why is it, then, that when it comes to getting full spiritually, we settle for half a cranberry?

Paul doesn't want that for us, and in this passage he reminds us that in Christ we have all we need to be all that God wants us to be.

Not infrequently you'll come across people who say either in word or deed that their lives are impoverished. Sometimes, remarkably, you'll find a believer who for some reason is looking for something else. He is not satisfied. She is not filled full.

Remember this: The extent to which you need something else to fill you full is the extent to which you find Christ deficient. If you find Christ deficient, then you have found something in contradiction of Scripture, which says that in Christ all the fullness of Deity resides in bodily form.

We've got to decide, Is it true that in Christ we have all that we need?

You'll find in the church today many people propagating all kinds of things that believers "need." Not infrequently these things that Christians "need" have exceedingly tenuous connections to Christ, "in whom all fullness dwells." As soon as someone tells you that you need this, that, and the other thing, ask yourself, *Is this in any way diverting my attention from Christ? Is there any sense in which this is perverting the gospel of Christ, which tells me all fullness is in him? If I get into this particular thing, will it in any way subvert the authority of Christ in my life?*

Beware! Scripture declares that in Christ is all fullness, and if you are related to him, you have been given all fullness. We don't need something super-added, extra-plus to Christ. What we need is to daily discover all that we already have in him.

How much have you eaten off of Christ's banquet table? How full are you?

> *Father, thank you that in Christ is all I need to live a life that pleases you. Please help me to take advantage of what is available to me.*

Greater Is He That Is in You

Christ . . . is the head over every power and authority. Colossians 2:10

There were teachers coming into Colosse who suggested that if God is Spirit (which is good) and man is matter (which is evil), the only way God and man could relate would be by all kinds of intermediaries between God and man so that, slowly and insidiously, it would be possible to construct a bridge.

Paul says, in effect, "OK, let's assume that there are all kinds of powers and authorities, all kinds of things out there we don't understand. There is one thing you need to know: Whatever and whoever they are, Christ is in control. He is head over every power and authority."

Paul didn't go in for all the magical stuff that many of his contemporaries were into, but he did realize there were supernatural things going on all around him which he couldn't see. He didn't buy into all the elaborate spiritual hierarchies that many pagans talked about, but he did preach about Christians being in a real battle with real evil spirits. He wasn't afraid of them, but neither did he play with them.

Some people ignore any thought of spiritual dynamics in our world. They rush headlong into all kinds of things that may have demonic connections. They scamper impulsively into things which not infrequently are rooted in the occult. Even Christians are so careless today that they play around in these things and don't seem to understand that they are very, very vulnerable when they do.

We must understand that we are rooted in Christ, the one in whom all fullness is found. He is in control of those things.

If we keep our eyes on him, we'll know victory over whatever powers come against us.

But we'll only share in that victory if we're full. Half-starved Christians who refuse to feast on Christ's bounty make poor soldiers against the demons of hell.

What can you do to be a better soldier in the spiritual battles that go on around you?

Thank you, Father, that no matter what spiritual forces surround me, I can always know that Christ is the greatest of them all, and he is available with all his power, and he is in control.

Away with the Old Life!

In him you were also circumcised, in the putting off of the sinful nature, not with a circumcision done by the hands of men but with the circumcision done by Christ, having been buried with him. Colossians 2:11-12

God's covenant with Abraham directed Abraham and his descendants to be circumcised as the outward and visible sign of an inward and spiritual relationship. Through the prophets God later explained that it wasn't enough to have an outward and visible sign if there wasn't an inward and spiritual reality. The prophets used to talk not just about being circumcised physically, but being circumcised in heart. Godly Israelites needed a spiritual, inner circumcision that matched up to the external symbol.

In the same way, Paul says, Christ has come and done away with the sinful nature, that tendency to sin that's in all of us. All of us have a tendency to sin. Christ can "circumcise" that tendency when we come to him.

That doesn't mean God takes away our ability to sin. Rather, he gives us the desire and the ability not to sin.

We may not utilize that ability; we may stifle that desire and go on with the old life. When that happens we veer off track and end up in all kinds of destruction.

Do you have a tendency to lust or greed? Do you have problems in telling the truth, in desiring righteousness? In Christ we have been circumcised! Sin has been put off! Learn to live in the reality of it.

But what does it mean when it says we have been buried with Christ? Those of you who have attended the burial service of a loved one know its sense of finality, its sense of termination. You stand around the graveside, and you see the casket containing the remains of your loved one. You know that very shortly it will be lowered into the ground and that will mean termination.

In England ropes are put through hoops on the casket's side, and family members actually lower the casket into the open hole in the ground. Then they take soil and begin to cover it. There is an awful sense of termination in burial.

When Paul says you were buried with Christ, he means your conversion terminated the old life. It came to an end. When you identified with Christ, you said goodbye to the old stuff.

Forget this, and there's a good chance you'll slip back into the old ways. You might be crucified and buried with Christ; in fact, you're dead, but unfortunately you won't lie down. Listen, you need to borrow a shovel.

What are some tendencies you have to sin that need to be put off or done away with in order for your old life to be truly buried?

Lord, thank you for giving me the desire and the ability not to fall into my natural tendencies to sin. Please help me to live the new life you have given me and to let the old life stay dead.

On with the New!

... buried with him in baptism and raised with him through your faith in the power of God, who raised him from the dead. Colossians 2:12

Some people assume that all you've got to do is be baptized and automatically these spiritual things happen. They want it done as soon as possible to their children. They want to bring infants to church for baptism so that magically, mystically, mechanically, the children get an eternal life insurance policy.

Clearly that's not right. Baptism is significant and important, but it is never a substitute for faith.

Some people, hearing this, say, "It's obvious, then, that you don't baptize little children. You wait until people have exercised faith, and then you baptize them on confession of faith. That way nobody gets confused that baptism substitutes for faith."

That's sound reasoning, but Paul does seem to suggest a link between circumcision and baptism.

Israelites were circumcised on their eighth day of life, before they could exercise any faith at all. Those who see baptism as the New Testament equivalent of circumcision firmly believe that infants of believing parents should be baptized. They see baptism as a sign that the child has entered into the new covenant in the same way that circumcision signified the entrance of an Israelite child into the old covenant. They know that every child must one day come to faith and show the inner reality of the external symbol. But they insist you should not for that reason deny them the outward symbol.

No matter which mode of baptism people use, it is never a substitute for heart discipleship. Paul makes this clear in the rest of verse 12, when he insists the key even to baptism is faith: "having been buried with him in baptism and raised with him through your faith . . . " Baptism unrelated to faith is an empty tradition. Baptism as an outward and visible sign of an inward and spiritual grace is profoundly significant.

So what is Paul saying here? He's saying that, one way or another, your baptism is an outward expression of the inward reality of your identification with Christ. You are united to Christ by faith and have died to all that he died to. You've been buried; you've terminated the old life.

Can you honestly say that in him you have been buried to the old life and with him you have been raised to newness of life? Can you say that because you have exercised faith in the God who raised Christ from the dead, the power that raised him from the dead is operative in your life, and you are alive in him? Paul says that's what circumcision means. That's what baptism entails.

What does baptism mean to you?

Father, thank you that the true baptism happens inside and is done by you. Please help me to live in the reality of what you have done in my life, to live in your strength that you have made available to me.

The Cross That Forgives

When you were dead in your sins and in the uncircumcision of your sinful nature, God made you alive with Christ. He forgave us all our sins. Colossians 2:13

Do you know any couples who can't seem to stop fighting? They kick, scratch, bite, bicker, insult, blame, and fume. They dredge up old hurts and fling them in each other's face.

I wish these couples could see the difference that forgiveness makes in a marriage. I wish they could see the couples who come into my office with grudges as big as elephants and leave with a flicker of old love restored. These restorations don't happen all the time, of course, but once in a while a couple will try forgiving each other. What a thrill it is for a pastor to see forgiveness bring life and laughter to marriages that once were dead and full of hate.

Forgiveness. What a beautiful word, and how much we all stand in need of it! Not only in our marriages, but wherever people are involved. Without it, life is harsh, bitter, cold, and dreadful—in a word, hopeless.

"Hopeless" describes exactly our position prior to the cross. Before the cross, we were bitterly at odds with God. He would reach out in love, and we'd bite, scratch, kick, and insult. Then Calvary came, and God offered us forgiveness in Christ. His forgiveness allowed a real love affair to begin.

Christian, never forget: In Christ we have been forgiven. In verse 14 Paul talks about the code that was canceled. Think of the Ten Commandments. Think of how often you've broken them. Think of the things you've done that you shouldn't have. Think of all the things that you could have done that you haven't. Visualize, if you can, God making out your bill. Take a good, long, hard look . . . and declare bankruptcy. No way can you pay that bill.

Here is the great news: Jesus Christ took the bill to the cross, and stamped across it, "Paid in Full." That's what forgiveness means. He has canceled the debt. He has paid it in full. You are no longer bankrupt in the courts of heaven.

Are there any relationships in your life that seem hopeless and need forgiveness? How can your understanding of Christ's forgiveness help in those situations?

Father, thank you for not holding anything against me and for paying the price for the things I have hurt or broken. Please help me to be willing to do the same in the relationships you have given me.

The Cross That Liberates

He . . . canceled the written code, with its regulations, that was against us and that stood opposed to us; he took it away, nailing it to the cross.
Colossians 2:13-14

The cross means not only that Christ died for us, but that we died with him. It means that I died to all that Christ died for.

When Paul talks about us dying with Christ, he doesn't mean we are dead. He doesn't mean those things are dead. He just means that the relationship has been terminated.

I can still visualize one of the happiest days of my life. I was standing on parade in my Royal Marine uniform. The officer announced, "David Stuart Briscoe, you are now temporarily dismissed from His Majesty's Royal Marines and may, if you wish, seek civilian employment. But if you desire to sign on for another seven years, we'll be happy to entertain you."

I desired very much not to sign on for an additional seven years. I was free!

There was a gentleman there called the Regimental Sergeant Major. He had an immaculate uniform, a big voice, and a big mouth.

Whenever we saw him coming, our backs would spring up straight. We'd swing our arms to the shoulder, thumb on top, heels dug in. That's what you did when the RSM showed up.

The day I was released I saw the RSM walking toward me. My head sprang up, my back straightened, I began to march. My arm went to leap up to salute . . . and a little voice inside me said, *You died to him.*

And I said, *What?*

You died to him.

But he's not dead!

That's right, and you're not dead, either.

Well, if he's not dead, and I'm not dead, how could I have died to him?

Simple. You have no further obligation to him, and he has no further authority over you. So if you'd like, you can go on marching around like that, swinging your arm up to salute. You'll look very funny, but go right ahead if you want to. But why continue in subjection to that to which you died?

So a very funny thing happened. My back curled ever so slightly, my hands found their way deliciously into my pockets—they had not been there for two long years—I scuffed my heels, and as I walked past the man, I whistled.

He went red, turned to purple, then turned to puce. He couldn't do a thing.

That's what the Cross means. You died to all that it was necessary for Christ to die for. Why go on in bondage to it? You don't have to be. You're free! You've been liberated from all the hurtful things that would take your eyes off Christ.

The next time they come your way, just whistle at 'em. They can't do a thing.

What former slave owners can you now whistle at because of what Christ has done in setting you free?

Father, thank you that I no longer have any obligation to the things that used to or would control me if I didn't belong to you.

Meditations on Living like Christ

1. Read slowly through Romans 5:1-11, thinking about all that believers have to be joyful about.

2. Ephesians 1:3-14 lists several blessings believers have been given through Christ. Read the passage aloud several times in the next few weeks, in different translations, if you can. Each time, pray through the passage, thanking the Lord for all he has given us in Christ.

3. Read through 1 Thessalonians 4:1-12 a few times and reflect on the connection between what we believe and how we live.

4. What does 1 Peter 1:13-25 say about how we can become pure and holy?

5. 1 John 5:13 says that the entire book was written "so that you may know that you have eternal life." The book gives several ways we can know if someone is truly a believer. As you read through 1 John, list the characteristics of true children of God.

Where Am I Heading?

I'm hoping you have started out well in the Christian faith. I hope you've got solidly in mind the basics that will carry you through whatever hardships you may encounter in your spiritual walk. You've begun a fantastic journey that leads to unimaginable glory—but to reach that goal, you've got to stay in the race.

That's what Paul talked about in Colossians 1:23, which begins with an ominous little word—*if*. Such a little word, but one that causes great consternation.

To get the full impact of the verse, we need to return to verse 22: "But now he has reconciled you by Christ's physical body through death to present you holy in his sight, without blemish and free from accusation, *if you continue in your faith, established and firm, not moved from the hope held out in the gospel*" (vv. 22-23, emphasis added).

Paul is talking here about what's often called "the perseverance of the saints." He wants us to understand that those who are reconciled and justified will continue in the faith.

How can you tell if a person is a real Christian? All kinds of tests are often given, but Paul said that those who are truly justified and reconciled persevere; they continue in the faith. They are like a solid building on a good foundation. They are not easily moved away. They are loyal to the faith. They finish their race.

They have their eyes fixed on the hope that is in the gospel. They have an objective to reach, and they dedicate themselves to reaching it. They are utterly convinced of the faith, confident in it. They keep on keeping on.

They didn't make a snap decision about following God and then forget him. They didn't say, "Sure, I'm a Christian," and then go on living in the old way, uninterested in living Christianly.

Those who are truly justified and reconciled are loyal, confident, convinced, growing, and progressing. How much we need to encourage one another in understanding this point!

F. F. Bruce, a British theologian, said, "Continuance [in the faith] is the test of reality."

How do you match up? Can you look back and say, "Because of all that Christ did on the cross, and because I placed my faith in his finished work, I have been reconciled to God. I have been justified, and I am determined, by God's grace, to continue in the faith. I'm thankful, and I intend to demonstrate my thankfulness by continuing to follow Christ"?

Christian brother or sister, the gospel's promise is too great and its prize too precious for you to drop out of the race now. Paul himself—no stranger to suffering, ridicule, and heartache—wrote, "I consider that our present sufferings are not worth comparing with the glory that will be revealed in us" (Rom. 8:18).

So hang in there! Continue what you started! By doing so, you not only prove the reality of your faith, but guarantee for yourself a prize, a trophy that no shelf on earth could possibly hold up.

Power to Persevere

Being strengthened with all power according to his glorious might so that you may have great endurance and patience. Colossians 1:11

We Christians aim at such an extraordinary goal that if we couldn't count on some help to reach it, we'd have no hope of succeeding.

Not only can we count on "some help," Paul says—we have available to us the very strength that birthed the stars and flung them out into the galaxies!

How great is this power available to us? If God's might were only as great as our need, or as great as our imagination, what a puny, limited God he would be! No, it is not according to human need or imagination, but in accordance with his majesty and glory.

Just imagine what a challenge it would be to say to yourself, "My purpose in life is to be worthy of Christ and to remember whom I represent. So I'm committed to please him at all times, by a life that practically demonstrates what he is doing within me. I will discover more and more of him, and I will reach my goal because of all his mighty power working in me." The picture of fulfillment he promises is simply staggering.

Notice, however, that this power is not there so that you will be able to do all kinds of fabulous, amazing, spectacular things so that people say, "Wow! That's power!"

No, it's amazingly down-to-earth. We are strengthened so that we might have endurance and patience. You can't get more practical than that.

The power of God is made available to people in superlative measure in order that they might live purposefully and powerfully down here in the normal circumstances of life. Endurance means responding properly to our external circumstances, having the strength to finish the race and win the prize.

Are external pressures so heavy upon you that you'd like to bury your head in the sand? Are you captivated by a desire to head for the bushes, escape to the mountains, get away from it all?

That's the normal approach, but it's not the one of a person discovering fulfillment. The person discovering fulfillment is in touch with the power of God, power that equips him to endure the difficult circumstances of life.

If you're to live in your circumstances, you'll also need patience. Patience is the power to restrain yourself. It's the ability to handle not the external circumstances, but those things that boil up within you. Patience allows you to control lust, greed, anger, malice, jealousy, all the things that erupt when we look for fulfillment in the wrong place.

God says, "You can be strengthened according to the might of my glory so that you'll have endurance to cope with your external circumstances and the patience to deal with your inner passions!"

When that kind of power is in your life, you begin to discover fulfillment.

Which do you struggle more with, your external circumstances or your inner passions? What is the significance of God's promise to you?

Father, thank you that you have promised us your power so that we can have all the endurance and all the patience we need to live a life that is pleasing to you.

The Joy of It All

. . . joyfully giving thanks to the Father, who has qualified you to share in the inheritance of the saints in the kingdom of light. Colossians 1:11-12

Notice that Paul doesn't talk just about the power of endurance and the power of patience. If he'd done that, he'd have sounded just like a Stoic philosopher. There are plenty of Stoics around. Stoics believe that you should endure everything and be patient about everything, that you should grit your teeth and bear it.

I always think of a Stoic when I see Robert Parrish play for the Boston Celtics. They call him "The Chief." He stands about seven feet tall, handsome, with finely chiseled features, his face betraying no emotion whatsoever. You could never tell if they were on top of the league or at the bottom, if he'd just lost his best friend or had just gotten married.

He's a born Stoic. I'll bet he can endure. I'll bet he's patient. But on the court he looks miserable.

Paul says that when you are strengthened with God's might, you will have great endurance and patience—but joyfully!—"joyfully giving thanks to the Father, who has qualified you to share in the inheritance of the saints in the kingdom of light."

That's the difference between striving for the prize of the gospel and straining for one that's temporal. You can win an earthly marathon with a grimace on your face and wind up with nothing more than a faded bauble to put on your mantle. But you win the race of the gospel with a smile on your lips and joy in your heart, for you know that you've been qualified to receive the eternal reward of a limitless inheritance.

And you know the best thing of all? In the Christian race, God himself hands out the medals.

If you were to rate yourself on a scale of one to ten, one being Stoic and ten being full of joy, how would you rate, and why?

Father, please help me to remember that the prize I am striving for is an eternal one, and one that I'll receive from you.

That Will Be Perfect!

We proclaim him, admonishing and teaching everyone with all wisdom, so that we may present everyone perfect in Christ. To this end I labor, struggling with all his energy, which so powerfully works in me.
Colossians 1:28-29

When we come to Christ, we don't just look in the past and say, "I feel good about myself." We must look to the future and say, "Where on earth is all this going?"

There is an end, an objective, a consummation of our faith. And we must live in the light of it at all times.

Back in verse 23 Paul talked about "the hope held out in the gospel." Then in verse 27 he talks about "the hope of glory." That word *hope* is the dominant theme of the Christian gospel. There's no Good News if there is no hope. Hope is something that people in all generations and all cultures look for.

Well, what is the world coming to? What's going to happen to me? Is there any hope?

"Yes!" the Scripture shouts. Tremendous hope is locked up in the gospel for every believer—the hope of glory.

The hope of glory means we know that when we die, we will be raised to new life as a result of Christ's resurrection, and we will see God in all his glory.

The end of our faith will be that we will not only see the glory of God, we will share in it for all eternity.

When I'm dead, I'm not done with. I will die in Christ, be raised in him, and share in his glory. That's the hope of the gospel. That is the hope of glory.

Paul also talks about the promise of perfection. He says the day is coming when we will be holy, blameless, faultless—perfect in God's sight.

There is a sense in which we are justified to that position right now. But on that day it will become actual. As a Christian, I am as justified now as I ever will be. I'm as holy and blameless in God's sight as I'll ever be.

But practically I'm not holy. My behavior is not blameless. Practically you could bring all kinds of accusations against me.

A day is coming when we will be perfected practically. We will stand before God without a hint or trace of anything of which we could be accused. When Christ appears, then we will appear with Christ in glory. Then we'll be perfect.

If we know that's where we're going, and if we know where we are, we will want to keep progressing in our experience of Christ so there are fewer and fewer things of which we can be accused.

We must live in the light of where we were, grateful that we're no longer there. We must continue in the light of where we are, concerned that we're still not what we ought to be. And we must press on to know Christ more fully, assured that one day we will stand before God clothed in perfect holiness.

That is where our faith is leading. It's a trip that promises great reward.

As you look back at your life, where were you? Where are you today? And where are you going, as you look ahead to the future?

Father, thank you for accepting and loving me completely just as I am now, and for seeing me as perfect in Christ. And thank you that someday I will stand before you absolutely pure and holy, because of your Son.

Savior and Lord

So then, just as you received Christ Jesus as Lord, continue to live in him. Colossians 2:6

When we talk about receiving Christ in our modern setting, we often think in terms of "asking Jesus into our heart." Too often the concern is merely to get people to respond with the heart rather than the mind.

I suspect that when Paul talked about receiving Christ Jesus as Lord, he expected those he was evangelizing first of all to receive the truth of Christ. And when you look at how Paul writes to new believers, you cannot escape one thing: New believers in Paul's day were well taught in Christian theology.

He also says that they received Christ Jesus as Lord. Not infrequently you'll hear people say things like, "I received Jesus as my Savior at such-and-such a time, but it wasn't until x number of years later that I received him as my Lord."

I understand what people mean by that. They mean that they started off on their pilgrimage and only later had a deeper experience. I don't have any problems with that. But I do have problems with their terminology.

I don't know how you can receive Jesus without receiving Jesus Christ the Lord. You cannot separate them. Paul is crystal clear at this point. "You received Christ Jesus as Lord."

Look at it this way. You want Jesus to save you from death, hell, and the devil, but how can he save you from what he hasn't conquered? But if he has mastered these things in order to save you from them, it's because he is Lord of them. Therefore, the idea of him saving you presupposes his lordship.

If the one I am receiving into my life is the Lord, and I recognize that it is only his Lordship that qualifies him to be my Savior, how can I receive him without acknowledging his mastery of my life? I can't.

I'm not saying you have to understand all the ramifications of lordship or that you've got to be "totally surrendered" (whatever that is). But people who casually bow their heads and say a little prayer without any deeper understanding of Christ or any readiness to submit their lives to him are people who have not adequately seen Christ Jesus as Lord.

What does it mean to receive Jesus Christ as Lord?

Father, please help us to more clearly understand what it means to have a Savior who is Lord of all he saves me from, and also Lord of me.

Bloom Where You're Planted

Continue to live in him, rooted and built up in him, strengthened in the faith as you were taught, and overflowing with thankfulness.
Colossians 2:6-7

Sometimes the Milwaukee Bucks frustrate me. They'll start out a game with a rush and find themselves up by twenty points. Then somebody, somewhere, suggests they "protect the lead."

You know what happens. They change tactics, deviating from the way they began, and soon they're in deep, deep trouble.

The Bucks aren't the only ones liable to do this sort of thing. Most athletic teams, and we Christians, are prone to falling into the same trap. We trust Christ to be our Lord and Savior, and somewhere along the way we change tactics. We forget how we began. And then we're in trouble.

Paul encourages believers to continue in their walk with the Lord the same way they began. To do that, we've got to be clear how we started. Notice how Paul said it: "Just as you received Christ Jesus as Lord, continue to live in him." The word translated "live" here is really the word for "walk." I start out by acknowledging his mastery. I acknowledge his rule one step at a time. When that happens, I begin to bloom where I'm planted.

Can you think of anyone who is not blooming, or looks kind of withered? They need a ministry of encouragement. "Or maybe that's what's wrong with me," you say. "I remember getting planted, and I remember receiving Christ, but I guess I didn't continue as I started. I guess I didn't bloom where I was planted."

Be encouraged. Press on! And you do that by developing as you are instructed, Paul says—being "strengthened in the faith as you were taught."

If you started out being taught Christ Jesus as Lord, don't deviate from that. It's basically all you need to know. All kinds of people will come with all sorts of other stuff, but don't move one inch from the fundamental truth that you were taught: Christ Jesus as Lord. You received Christ Jesus as Lord. Now continue as you started. Bloom where you're planted. Be "strengthened . . . as you were taught."

Finally, Paul says, make sure you are overflowing with thanksgiving. The picture here is of a river overflowing its banks.

When you go deep in Christ, get involved in a group that encourages you, and start encouraging others, you'll have so much to be thankful for that your banks will overflow. And you'll find people gathering around those banks to be encouraged themselves. Then you can all bloom together.

Do you know someone who needs to be encouraged? What can you do to help?

Father, I want to acknowledge your lordship in every little step I take today. Please help me to be especially conscious of you today, and aware of what you want me to do.

To Be or Not to Be

When Christ, who is your life, appears, then you also will appear with him in glory. Colossians 3:4

One of the most famous things that Paul ever said challenged me as a teenager. It became so powerful in my thinking that I never got away from it. This is what he said: "For to me to live is Christ, and to die is gain." Think of that!

Do you remember when Hamlet said, "To be or not to be, that is the question"? Life was so unbearable for him that he was thinking of ending it, but the thought of ending it was even more unbearable.

The apostle, I think, could have said the same thing: "To be or not to be, that is the question." He would have meant just the opposite of what Hamlet did, however. "If I go on being," I can hear him say, "In Christ I have all I need for any eventuality. I've been thrown in prison, beaten up, bitten by snakes, maltreated, stoned. But Christ is my life in all these things. For to me to live is Christ, and to die is gain."

Why would dying be a gain? Because he enjoyed Christ down here even with stonings and snake bites. When he died and went to heaven he would enjoy Christ minus stonings and snake bites. The key here or there was that Christ was his life. Other things were incidental.

There are some people whose lives are governed by stonings and snake bites, and others whose lives are governed by Christ, who is their life. If we belong to the second group, we'll be excited to hear that "when Christ, who is your life, appears, then you also will appear with him in glory."

The risen Christ, ascended to the Father's right hand, will come in glorious majesty. What a turning point in history that will be!

Some think history simply lurches from one event to another. They look at events and see no rhyme nor reason to them. They see history as one tragedy or disaster heaped upon another, believe everything is a mess, and wonder what on earth will happen next.

Others see history as moving in cycles. They say that if we just hang in there, we'll come around the corner eventually.

Still others see history moving relentlessly toward God's foreordained conclusion.

What is your approach to history? Mine is that Christ, seated at the Father's right hand, is life, and one day when God says, "Enough is enough," Jesus Christ will appear in glory to be hailed as King of kings and Lord of lords. Those who are Christ's will appear with him, glorified, and will share in his glory.

That's where history is going.

What do life and death mean to you?

Father, thank you that Christ will always be our life, and because of him, you will be with us through life and through death.

What Needs to Go?

Put to death, therefore, whatever belongs to your earthly nature: sexual immorality, impurity, lust, evil desires and greed, which is idolatry. Because of these, the wrath of God is coming. Colossians 3:5-6

Because of all the sin and wickedness mentioned in verse 5, the wrath of God is coming.

We get a little mealy-mouthed about this aspect of Christian truth. It's true that God is a God of infinite love, grace, and mercy. It's also true he's a God of infinite holiness and purity. That means he must reward what is right and punish what is wrong.

That means I need to identify those areas in my life that violate what I profess. If Christ is my life, how can I be dominated by anything else? How can he become peripheral? If Christ is my life, why do all kinds of opinions, movements, and trends make more of an impact on me than what Christ has said? Why do they move me more than what Christ has promised?

When I start thinking it through, I realize I need to apply and obey this truth. When I look carefully at verse 5, three words leap out: *immorality, impurity,* and *idolatry.* These must be dealt with by God's people, and the treatment must be radical. Put them to death.

Some researchers estimate that 50 percent of American women and 70 percent of American men commit adultery. We are an adulterous generation.

God calls adultery sexual immorality, and he says it is totally incompatible with Christian profession. It is totally inappropriate, and if you are into it—and chances are that I am addressing people even at this moment who are sitting comfortably in an easy chair, planning to commit adultery before the next devotion—I warn you to cut it out! Put it to death! It is completely unacceptable.

Why? Because Christ is your life, you are bound up with him, and you are planning to appear with him in glory. When he comes in glory, he will judge everyone who does these things.

Impurity and idolatry are just as unacceptable as immorality. You say, "You're not going to accuse us of idolatry now, are you? You don't really think we've got little statues carved out of wood to which we bow down and offer bowls of rice?"

No, I don't. Idolatry is much more than that. Whatever I am absorbed with, whatever demands most of my time, begins to rule my life. Anything that takes God's place in my life is an idol. "The dearest idol I have known, whatever that idol be, help me to tear it from thy throne, and worship only thee," says the old chorus.

"If there is an adulterous relationship in your life," Paul would say, "stop it! If your life is becoming obsessed and absorbed by the inappropriate or the unacceptable, make some radical changes. Your life depends upon it!"

"When Christ, who is your life, appears, then you also will appear with him in glory" (Col. 3:4). That is where your life is heading. That is what you have to look forward to.

Make sure that when that day arrives, it will be a day of rejoicing and glad shouting, and not a day of shame and tears.

What is it that absorbs most of your time and attention lately? Can you see any signs that this is ruling your life?

Father, I bring to you today the things that are important to me. Please sort them out for me and show me your priorities for my life.

Meditations on Our Destination

1. Read through 1 Corinthians 9:24-27, thinking about the similarities between the Christian life and athletics. What does this imply about how we ought to live? How do you respond to Paul's example in 2 Timothy 4:6-8?

2. Copy Hebrews 10:35-39 on an index card or a small piece of paper and put it up on your mirror or somewhere you will be able to look at it and think about it often. How can this encourage you to persevere?

3. Slowly read 2 Peter 3:3-15 aloud to yourself every morning for a week or two. How does this encourage us to be holy and godly?

How Should I Act?

Wouldn't it be interesting if, when you became a Christian, God said, "My objective is to get you to heaven, so why don't I take you now?"

One problem with that is that we'd delay becoming Christians as long as possible so we could have as much "fun" down here as we could, then get saved and be wafted off to heaven.

God, however, decided not to do it that way. It is down here, with our two big feet squarely planted in the middle of a secular society, that our Christianity is to be lived. Christians have always had to apply themselves to the culture in which they are planted.

There was a time in my life when I had to determine how I was going to live as a Christian in wartime Britain. Our culture was quite clearly drawn. There was a unique set of circumstances which I had to confront.

Later I had to ask myself how a Christian should behave as a Royal Marine, in an entirely different culture. Subsequently I moved to the United States and found myself in a middle-class suburb of old Milwaukee and had to ask, What does it mean to be a Christian in this new culture?

The easy thing would be to conform to the prevailing culture and put our Christianity on the shelf, but we're not free to do that. We have to examine our culture in the light of Christianity, stand firm on Christian principles, and challenge our culture to adapt. That's what it means to be godly.

Godliness has a spiritual dimension that is essentially practical. It produces things. It's down-to-earth, solid. A life of faith expresses itself in what it does. It can't just put on a show.

If you were to come to my house, I would offer you some fruit. I have a beautiful carved dish from the Venezuelan jungle. It's carved in solid, heavy black timber in the shape of a leaf. On it are the brightest, most beautiful apples you ever saw. I would welcome you and invite you to take one.

I have enormous fun doing that, because for years I've been giving away those apples. The same apples. You see, they're made of the same wood as the dish, and you can't tell it until you try to bite into one.

You can carve wood to look like fruit, but that's not fruit. Fruit is the natural product of the healthy tree, the external evidence of inward vitality.

Spiritual fruit is the natural product of a healthy faith, the external evidence of a vital internal life. Our faith motivates us to serve God and others, and to be loving, giving people. We do it for the Lord, and we're rewarded with fulfilled lives.

Unfortunately, people hell-bent on personal satisfaction won't believe that. "I've had it up to here with giving," they say, "and with being driven to exhaustion serving God and serving people. I'm going to please myself from now on." A sad commentary on the experience of many Christians is that they decided to go so far and no further. "That's it," they say, and they never progress an inch.

But the fruitful life progressively makes new discoveries of God and enjoys a new devotion to God. It is progress, growth, development.

If I ever sense that my discovery of God has ground to a halt, if I ever discover that my devotion to God has reached a plateau, then I can be absolutely certain that my life is being filled with things that will never provide fulfillment.

Do you want to be fulfilled? Then discover for yourself what a life of fruitfulness has to offer. And stay away from wooden apples!

A Drink That Satisfies

We have heard of your faith in Christ Jesus and of the love you have for all the saints. Colossians 1:4

Occasionally after one of our church services people will stand in the foyer, look across the crowd, and see a former college classmate. "I don't believe it," they'll gasp. "Look at him. I remember what he used to get into when he . . . ha ha ha, hee hee, oh, he's the last person . . ."

They make their way across the foyer, compare notes, and discover that the other person was thinking exactly the same thing about them. They discover that even though they were into all kinds of junk way back then, somewhere along the line they came to faith in Christ Jesus, their life was changed, and they've become holy and faithful brethren in Christ.

It was like that in Colosse. Everybody knew everyone else's background; nevertheless there was a genuine, loving concern for one another.

In Colosse they had probably known each other since they were knee high to a grasshopper. They'd known everything that everybody had gotten into. There were no secrets. It had a small town mentality, a small town involvement. The gospel had come in, and the most unlikely people had believed.

Their problems were compounded because some of the church's members were Jews and some were Gentiles, some were slaves and some were slave owners, some were men and some were women. Many in these groups detested each other externally, but they learned to love each other in Christ despite their suspicions and animosities.

Why? Because the apostle Paul taught that in Christ all these barriers and sociological chasms had been bridged. They could now begin to live as one body. They began to love each other, and outsiders noticed.

"Something's going on here," they said.

"What's going on," the Christians said, "is that God has worked in our lives and has brought us to faith in Christ, and he's encouraging us and enabling us to love the saints."

The key to this love is found in the very last expression of Colossians 1:8, where Paul talks about their love "in the Spirit."

Let's face it, as a friend of mine used to say, "God must love strange people—he sure made plenty."

No doubt you've heard it said that often it's harder to get along with God's people than it is to get along with pagans. Frankly, I've said it. I've got some pagan friends with whom I never have a wrong word. But with some Christians . . .

The point is that there's every possibility for things going wrong unless the Spirit of God works in our hearts. When we allow the Spirit to work in our hearts, not only can he bring us to faith in Christ, but he can actually bring us to love the saints.

That's what Paul was so grateful for. He could see it happening in the church at Colosse.

If the great apostle were alive today, would he see it happening in our churches? If he showed up at this Sunday's services, would he come away grateful to God for the loving attitudes and actions of the people that he saw there?

Or better yet: If he visited our homes and businesses this week, during the busiest part of the day, would he give thanks for the acts of love he saw Christians bestow upon one another?

When we respond to our Lord's call for Christians to love one another, this old world will get a glorious taste of the delicacies of heaven. The elixir of love is irresistible.

Can thirsty souls get a drink from your cup?

How have you experienced this love? How have you given it?

Father, thank you for giving us this love, and for how it draws people to you. Please help us to give it away more and more, so others will see how it satisfies.

A Twelve-Lane Highway

Since the day we heard about you, we have not stopped praying for you and asking God to fill you with the knowledge of his will through all spiritual wisdom and understanding. Colossians 1:9

A knowledge of God's will is one thing no believer can do without. Paul was convinced that his Colossian friends had to have it.

We must have it, too. When we are filled with that knowledge, spiritual wisdom and understanding are the natural overflow.

Paul is not saying that he wants each of the Colossians to know intellectually what God's will is. You have to start there, but you've got to go much further than that. You have to act on what you know.

But even that is not enough. After you've discovered God's will and have done it, you must come to delight in it. When you do, you'll sense new direction. There'll be a purposefulness about your life—you'll discover what God wants you to be.

I don't mean that you'll know all the minute details of God's will for your life. I'm not so sure God is concerned about all the minute details. I worry when people talk about God's will as if it were a high wire, easy to topple off if you're not careful to keep your balance.

God's will isn't a high wire. God's will is a 12-lane highway. He's got you and me going in a certain direction, and the varieties of possibility are boundless.

To be filled with the knowledge of God's will doesn't mean you've got to know absolutely everything about everything, that you must know what God wants you to do at every moment in every circumstance. That's not it.

On the other hand, Paul does want us to understand that God has a plan for our lives, a good, acceptable, and perfect plan. We discover what it is in general terms from Scripture. When we do what it requires of us, increasingly we'll delight in it.

As a result, we gain spiritual wisdom—not street smarts, but spiritual wisdom and understanding, which inform us of the spiritual realities in our lives. We're in tune with heaven, we're in step with the Spirit. Therein, says Paul, is fullness of life.

How do you know what God's will is for your life?

Father, today I pray that you would help me know the general direction you want me to go.

A Walk That Pleases

And we pray this in order that you may live a life worthy of the Lord and may please him in every way: bearing fruit in every good work, growing in the knowledge of God. Colossians 1:10

What if I've decided what I want to do with my life, and I've been happy doing my own thing? And what if suddenly God blows the whistle and says, "Foul!"

Do I start yelling at the umpire? Or do I say, "Okay," and ask myself, *What did I do wrong?* The answer will come loud and clear: "You weren't interested in doing God's will, therefore you haven't taken time to discover what it is. You've only been interested in doing your own thing, and have expected God to smile benignly upon you and bless you out of your socks."

If that's what's wrong, I've got to go back to the drawing board and decide if I'm going to find out what God's will is and walk with him. Only when I do that can I enjoy a life of purposefulness. My new, overriding purpose will be to "live a life worthy of the Lord." What does that mean?

The word translated *live a life* is actually the Greek word for *walk*. The Christian life is frequently described as a walk. It gives the idea of progression and reminds us that it is lived one step after another. It's not just one big step. We don't become perfect immediately. But when I know I represent my Lord, when I know that in some way my conduct is tied to the glory of his person, I'll be careful. I don't want my behavior to reflect negatively on him.

Some people take a step into Christ and they stop. They're stuck. You come across them years later, and they haven't gotten anywhere.

Those who are living a life worthy of the Lord are progressively, situation by situation, circumstance after circumstance, doing and delighting in his will.

The king of England's two sons were in Hyde Park. The prince of Wales said to the duke of York, "I bet you a shilling that all fat policemen have bald heads." The duke said, "You're wrong."

Just then, a fat policeman came along on cue. They didn't know how to dislodge his helmet, but fortunately there was a little cockney kid from the east of London nearby. They said to him, "I say, old fellow" (that's how king's sons tend to speak), "We'll give you a shilling if you can dislodge that officer's helmet."

"I'll do it for nothing," he answered.

He picked up a stone and threw it . . . bulls-eye! Off came the helmet. Sure enough, he had a bald head. The prince turned to the duke of York and said, "You owe me a shilling."

They were settling their debts and their winnings when the portly officer descended upon them, grabbed the boys, and in typical police fashion, got out his little notebook, licked his pencil, and said, "What are your names?"

"Prince of Wales," said the first boy.

"First you assault my person, then you insult my uniform!" the officer snarled. "I could have you on charges for this. What's your name?"

"I really am the prince of Wales," came the reply.

"What's your name, then?" he asked the second boy.

"I am the duke of York," the boy said.

"I don't believe you, either." Turning to the third scruffy little kid, he asked, "And what's your name?"

At this the lad nudged the other two and said, "I'm the archbishop of Canterbury."

The problem with claiming to be the prince of Wales when you go around knocking off policemen's helmets is that nobody believes you. A noble status demands a disciplined life. Christians find fulfillment and purpose in living a life worthy of the Lord.

When we do that, we can't help pleasing him.

I don't know about you, but my greatest ambition in life is to enjoy the smile of his approval. A grin like his can keep me going for eternity!

Do you consciously try to know and do God's will, or do you tend to do your own thing and hope he will like it?

Father, please help my walk today to be worthy of you.

A Heart in Heaven

Set your hearts on things above, where Christ is seated at the right hand of God. Colossians 3:1

It's fun watching young men in love. It can be even more fun when the romance is long distance.

You can predict what will happen. There'll be hours of late-night, heart-pounding telephone conversations. The postal service will be overrun with love notes crossing each other in the mail. Pillows will be soaked with tears.

But the most telling symptom is the glazed, faraway look in Romeo's eyes. I'm sure you've seen it. You ask the man a question and you get a blank stare. He's not at home. He's elsewhere, in another land. He's with his sweetheart.

You might say his heart is set on things afar, where Juliet is seated right by the telephone.

Colossians 3:1 has something much grander in view than young love, but perhaps this can get us in the right frame of mind. "Set your hearts on things above, where Christ is seated at the right hand of God," Paul says. But before we can understand how to do that, we need to look at the truth that is being stated here: "Christ is seated at the right hand of God."

We all understand that the Bible teaches the Lord Jesus Christ was with the Father before the worlds were made. We know that he assumed our humanity, was born a baby in Bethlehem, lived on earth for about thirty-three years, died an ignominious death, on the third day rose again from the dead, ascended to the Father, and is now seated at the Father's right hand.

Those are basic Christian truths. This is Christian theology. As we are exposed to these pieces of information, we determine whether they are true or false. If it is true that Christ is seated at the Father's right hand, that means death did not conquer him, but he conquered death. It means the risen Lord Jesus is greater than everything that ever defeated a human being, in him all authority resides, and through him alone can sinful mankind hold audience with God the Father. All that is contained in the statement, "Christ is seated at the right hand of God."

How does the truth that "Christ is seated at the right hand of God" make us want to set our hearts on things above?

Thank you, Father, for giving me something and someone so wonderful to set my heart and mind on.

This World Is Not My Home

Since, then, you have been raised with Christ, set your hearts on things above, where Christ is seated at the right hand of God. Colossians 3:1

It's one thing for me to believe that Jesus Christ, risen from the dead, is seated at the Father's right hand. It's an entirely different thing to see how that has an impact on my own life.

In some way, Paul says, I have been raised with Christ. In other words, my life is inextricably bound up in his life. His life is inextricably bound up in mine. In God's way of looking at things, I am locked into Christ—the same Christ who has ultimate authority and immediate access to the Father. Because I am related to him, I enjoy the same access!

If this is true, then some phenomenal things have taken place. "Wow!" I say, "if Christ is seated at the Father's right hand, and I am locked up in him, then heaven is really my home and earth is only my temporary residence!"

That's the reverse of what we normally think. We tend to think that earth is where the action is and heaven is a dull place way out there somewhere, to be dodged as long as possible. We tend to think that life is all about what we can see, touch, taste, and feel. We think it's earthy.

But Scripture tells us that if Christ is seated at the Father's right hand and my life is locked up in him, then heaven is my true home and my sojourn here is temporary. That changes my whole orientation to life.

If Christ is seated at the Father's right hand, and I have been raised with him, then eternity is the ultimate reality and time is merely transient. That, too, is exactly the opposite of what we tend to think. Our natural tendency is to assume that time is where it's at. "You only go around once in life, so grab for all the gusto you can," goes the ad slogan.

We may not drink their beer, but we listen to their commercials and to a large extent go along with them unthinkingly. We don't stop to realize that they wholly oppose Christian truth, which says what really matters is eternity, not time. What you've got here you will leave. Reality is found in eternity and heaven. That's what it means when it says Christ is seated at the Father's right hand and you have been raised with him.

What do you think of when you read that "you have been raised with Christ"?

Father, please help me not to unthinkingly go along with the world's mindset, but to remember that what really counts is what will last forever.

I'm Just a-Passin' Through

Since, then, you have been raised with Christ, set your hearts on things above. Colossians 3:1

Do you mean to tell me," you say, "that because I am united with Christ and because he was raised, that heaven is where I belong, earth is a temporary residence, eternity is where it's at, and time is fleeting?"

Yes. Emphatically yes! That's exactly what Paul means.

That being the case, there's a command we need to obey: "Set your hearts on things above." That doesn't make any sense at all until you understand the truth that is stated, then how that truth is applied. But when you do understand, it's nonsense not to obey.

If it is true that he is raised and I am in him, then my affections need to be locked into Christ, locked into the right hand of the Father, locked into heaven, and locked into eternity. That's where my heart really is. The Lord Jesus said, "Where your treasure is, there will your heart be also."

The converse is also true. Where your heart is, that's where your treasure is going to be.

So ask yourself a question: "Am I clear that Christ is at the Father's right hand? Do I understand that I, united with him, find my life where he is? And do I recognize that when my heart is seated in Christ at the Father's right hand, the place of authority and access to the Father, that eternity is reality and that heaven is my home?"

When I understand all these things, my heart says, *That's where I find my deepest desires*. We see everything in light of this.

Setting our hearts on things above presupposes that we'll guard our affections. How easily our affections can be infected! How often we see young people doing well spiritually until they reach that terribly vulnerable time when their affections start playing tricks on them. Having made a good profession of faith, they fall in love with someone who hasn't the slightest interest in Christ. And what happens? Christ is disregarded. He is disregarded because their affections are unguarded. I have seen it happen far too often.

If we are seated with Christ at the Father's right hand, we also need to guide our affections, to focus them on him, so that we understand the truth and tune in to the right wavelength.

Why do we need to guard and guide our affections? Because Christ is seated at the Father's right hand, and we are seated with him. Believe me, there's no better place to be.

How are you doing at guiding your affections toward Christ and what is eternal?

Father, thank you that you promised to help us guard our hearts. We really need your help to do what you ask.

Heavenly Minded

Set your minds on things above, not on earthly things. For you died, and your life is now hidden with Christ in God. Colossians 3:2-3

Albert Einstein had more trouble finding his way home from work than he did finding the key to atomic power.

One evening as he sat deep in thought aboard the train that brought him home each night, the porter approached to collect his ticket. Einstein rummaged around in his coat, through his pockets, in his shirt, and everywhere else he could think of. He grew alarmed at his inability to find the ticket.

"That's okay, Dr. Einstein," said the porter, "I know you ride this train every day. I can collect tomorrow."

"That's fine for you, young man," Einstein replied, "but how am I supposed to know where to get off the train without my ticket?"

Paul surely was as single-minded as Einstein, but he had a better idea of where he was going. He wanted his readers to join him in the trip. "Set your minds on things above," he writes.

"Hoo boy, these preachers, they do repeat themselves," you say. "He just said to set your hearts on things above, and now he says set your minds on things above."

But Paul is not repeating himself here. It's one thing to set your heart on things; it's another to set your mind on them. In this passage Paul makes a distinction between your affections and your grasp of truth.

What is the truth stated here? It's found in verse 3: "For you died, and your life is now hidden with Christ in God."

That's a truth, all right, but it's a little hard to grasp and a little harder to believe. What does he mean?

Let's back up a bit. Earlier in Colossians Paul insisted that not only did Christ die for us, but we died with him. Because it was necessary for Christ to die for some things, it is only appropriate that we should die to those same things.

If I know that I have done many evil and hurtful things in my life; if I am convicted that they are sin and I repent; if I ask forgiveness, understand that Christ died on the cross to forgive me and believe that I have been freely forgiven at the dreadful cost of Christ's life, then how could I merrily go back and engage in the evil that caused Christ's death?

When Paul says "you died," he is really saying that you cannot continue in those evil things because you are so thankful that Christ died to forgive you of them.

"Now, just a minute," you say. "If I walk away from all that I used to live for, what would I live for?"

The answer is in the second part of the passage: "Your life is now hidden with Christ in God."

How does the fact that "you died . . ." help you to set your mind on things above?

Father, you know I need your help to keep my mind set on "things above." Help me to think of what is eternal while time is flying by.

The Hidden Source

Your life is now hidden with Christ in God. Colossians 3:3

There is a secret in your life. This secret is not all the things you'd rather cover up, not all the things you used to get into, but a wondrously good thing that is hidden. It is hidden in God, and it has to do with Christ.

Have you ever met anybody whose life was hidden with Dow Jones in Wall Street? He can't wait to grab the paper in the morning, and you know exactly which page he'll turn to first. He'll do this even though he already knows how the Dow Jones did, because he listened to the news the night before.

Or take some teenagers. Without a constant fix of Tina Turner or the latest from Michael Jackson, they can't keep going. Their life is hidden with MTV.

In a similar way, Paul says Christians are caught up in who Christ is, what he says, and what he has promised. The secret, the source, and the content of their life are found in him. It's hidden, but it's where they belong. Christians died a radical termination of the old life. Their life is hidden with Christ in God.

How does that change things?

When your life is hidden with Christ in God, your life's center is Christ. The core of your existence is hidden—and you can prove it.

"My life was dependent on my business, then I lost my business. I walked away from it."

"My life was dependent on my family. Then my family let me down."

"I had all the money I needed, and I could buy whatever I wanted. But I'm afraid I made some bad investments, and it's all gone."

The remarkable thing is that some who have gone through similar experiences seem to keep on an even keel. You can chop away at their life—this goes, that goes—you keep chopping away, and you wonder, *When on earth will we get them?*

The answer is, you won't. You can touch all the earthly things, legitimate and illegitimate, but you can never destroy the center of their life for one simple reason: The center of their life is Christ.

That's why you'll find some people rotting in a cell in the Eastern bloc, without friends, without family, without church, without Bible, without hymn book, and you can't break their spirit. Their life is hidden with Christ in God.

Paul tells us to set our minds on things above, because the center of your life is locked up in Christ, and he is double-wrapped in God. Enemies can get you at any other point, but they can't touch you there.

Think of the worst thing that could happen to you. It's not difficult for any of us. We've all got our pet phobias. What if it happened?

If you're a Christian, you would be rocked, shaken, grief-stricken—but fundamentally you would be unmoved. Your life is hidden with Christ in God, and you have your mind set on him. People who get to that point are remarkable and unusual.

You've heard of people who are so heavenly minded they're no earthly good. Have you met anyone like that? I confess I haven't. Not a one. You see, that's not our problem today.

Our problem is that we are riddled with people who are so earthly minded they're no heavenly use. Paul is not being impractical when he talks about setting your minds on heaven. He's not unrelated to where life is. He knows you've got to live your life down here, and he doesn't promise God will lift you out of the whole thing.

What he insists is that the source and the core in the center of your life is found in Christ, not in earthly things. Therefore, whatever you do, don't allow your attention to be diverted from Christ.

Keep your eyes locked on him, obey what he has said, and you'll never have to worry about becoming so earthly minded you're of no heavenly use. You'll be the kind of person who's highly valued both on earth and in heaven.

And we can always use a few more of those.

Where is your life "hidden"?

Father, please help me be so deeply hidden in you that no matter what happens, the core of my being will be unshaken, grounded firmly in you.

Soar like an Eagle!

You used to walk in these ways, in the life you once lived. But now you must rid yourselves of all such things as these: anger, rage, malice, slander, and filthy language from your lips. Colossians 3:7-8

When Jack Eckerd, owner of the Eckerd Drug chain, became a Christian, he knew his life would never be the same. His employees discovered the same thing a short time later.

Chuck Colson relates how Eckerd once walked into one of his stores and spied some soft-core porno magazines for sale. His newly awakened conscience blared an alert, and he ordered his chief of operations to remove the offensive publications from all his stores.

"But Mr. Eckerd," the man said, "you don't know how much money those magazines bring in! Let me get some information together and show you tomorrow."

Early the next day, the man walked into Eckerd's office and showed him the figures. The magazines did earn a substantial profit.

"Take 'em out," Eckerd ordered. "That's an order."

Eckerd understood that when he came to Christ, he took off his old life as if it were an old garment, and threw it away. He put on a new garment, the righteousness of Christ.

When you asked to be forgiven of your sins, you put off the old life; it is unthinkable that you should have asked to be forgiven your sins if you intended to continue in them. You have taken off the old life like a dirty garment. You have thrown it away, stepped into the shower, and been cleansed by Christ. When you came out, you were dressed splendidly in a new wardrobe. Don't put your dirty old gear on top of it!

You are a new person. If that's true, then you need to clean up your personal and social life.

Do you know anyone who is given to fits of rage, anger, slander, and abusive language? It's obvious that such a person has all kinds of social problems.

One of the best mirrors of your spirituality is your social life. If you are being steered away into the kinds of activities where Christ is not welcome, that tells you something about your heart.

More than that—if your life is one ongoing fight, that tells you something about you. Not only is your heart wrong, but your mind is set on the wrong thing.

If that's true of you, take action. Clean it up. Get your act together. Why? Because you have taken off the old life and have put on the new.

Whatever is holding you down, put it where it belongs and begin to live in Christ.

What are some things that hold you back from soaring?

Father, please help me get rid of the old stuff that is left behind, and keep renewing me to bring me closer to your image.

People in Process

Do not lie to each other, since you have taken off your old self with its practices and have put on the new self, which is being renewed in knowledge in the image of its Creator. Colossians 3:9-10

All these changes won't come into your life overnight. Sometimes it takes awhile.

One day, about a hundred years ago, Phillips Brooks, the author of the Christmas carol "O Little Town of Bethlehem," was pacing fretfully in his office and muttering to himself. A friend walked into his study and asked what troubled him.

"The trouble is that I'm in a hurry, and God isn't," Brooks replied.

That's often our trouble, too. We want immediate action when God seems content to move slowly. Sometimes agonizingly so.

Have you ever noticed something like this? You think Mrs. Brown should have mastered by now a problem that's plagued her for years. Mrs. Brown thinks Mr. Smith should be ashamed of making so little progress in some other area. And Mr. Smith thinks that any real Christian ought to be able to tame a quick temper (like the one you've got).

People want change to come quickly—especially when it's change in someone else. But Paul says believers are a people in process. Believers have put on the new self "which is being renewed in knowledge in the image of its Creator." Notice the tense! While there is a very real sense in which Christians have been redeemed as an accomplished fact, there is another sense in which being renewed is a process. In terms of forgiveness, your salvation is complete; but in terms of being changed, your salvation is an ongoing procedure.

This is something that both Christians and critics of Christians sometimes misunderstand or ignore. Paul says being renewed requires time, and it will only be complete when believers stand before Christ. Scripture says when we stand before him we will see him and will be like him.

We need to understand this about ourselves and about each other. Do you know why? When we understand we're imperfect and incomplete and that we don't have it all together, it's amazing how tolerant we can become of each other. If we expect everybody to be perfect, to have it all together, and if we suggest we've already arrived, then there's no room for making mistakes and every excuse for being hard, harsh, unrelenting, and unforgiving.

On the other hand, if we know that we are people in process, then forgiveness, tolerance, and openness are in order. If it were not for this, it would be nonsense for Paul in verses 12-13 to talk about compassion, kindness, humility, gentleness, patience, bearing with each other, and forgiving one another.

Because we are people in process, we can respond to each other in gentleness and compassion. We should respect the struggle we're all going through. We should respect the aspirations we have but don't always achieve. We should remember that God is still working on us.

Some of us like bumper stickers. It seems to me that one of the most appropriate is surely "Please be patient, God isn't finished with me yet."

When you come across a group of believers that understands they are a people in process, you will find a congregation with a warm, generous spirit. If, on the other hand, you should uncover a group that doesn't appreciate the process, you're sure to find a spirit so hard and harsh as to shatter concrete. Or people.

If you are a believer, you are a person in process. As is every Christian you know. Do yourself a favor and treat others as the incomplete, maturing saints they are. Remember, God isn't finished with them yet.

Or with you!

How are you at remembering that all Christians are people in process?

Thank you, Father, that not only are you patient with us, but you also constantly work on us to make us more and more like you want us to be.

Meditations on Having a Christian Mind

1. Read through Matthew 5:43-48, thinking about what Christ asks us to do, how that will make us different from the rest of the world, and how he can expect so much of us. Then pray slowly through the passage, asking God to soften your heart toward those you have a hard time loving.

2. As you read and meditate on Galatians 5:13-15, ask yourself what freedom in Christ really means. How do we best demonstrate this freedom?

3. Read slowly through 2 Timothy 3:1-5. As we get nearer and nearer to the time of Christ's second coming, how difficult is it to live in a way that pleases God? How does our society today compare with how things will be in the "last days"? How should we respond?

4. Copy James 3:13-18 on a piece of paper and put it where you will see it every day for several weeks. Each time you see it, read it aloud and pray that God would help you to have this kind of wisdom, and that he would change you in one specific way that you notice during that particular reading.

5. Memorize 2 Peter 1:5-8, and try to keep it a part of your conscious memory during the day. Throughout each day, whenever you have time to think about it, whether in lines, in traffic, in a waiting room, or on a walk, think of ways you can do these things.

Who Can I Count On?

If you want to become a better basketball player, what do you do? You find a team and play on it.

If you want to learn Scandinavian cooking, what do you do? You find some old pros and imitate their technique.

If you want to grow as a parent, teacher, pianist, or manicurist, what do you do? You find people who have the same interest and long experience, and you spend time with them. That's how we grow in almost any field you can name.

So why is it that when it comes to spiritual growth, we abandon the process? Why is it that so many folks consider the church irrelevant to their spiritual growth and never see it as the fundamental, basic aspect of the process that it truly is? Their quest for spiritual maturity is stymied, but they never know why. It's really not such a mystery.

The fact is, if you want to grow, you must be involved in the church.

There are many pictures of the church in Scripture, but one of the best known and loved is of a body with Christ as its head. We are part of a fellowship where Christ is connecting all the members together, coordinating us, deeply involving us in the life of a believing fellowship under his control.

We dare not turn our eyes off Christ, but neither must we lose sight of the task to which Christ committed himself—the building of his church.

Christianity is not lived in isolation, "just me and the Lord." Christianity is lived within a community of believers. Every community must have a coordinated membership. Chaos results when everybody does his own thing.

Integrated, coordinated living in the fellowship of believers presumes that the people who would submit to the Lord also are prepared to submit to each other. It's at this very point that a lot of people in the church get into trouble.

When they find that things aren't going their way, they pick up their ball and head for another church. Instead of resolving the problem by displaying a submissive attitude, they simply take their rebellious disposition to another church. It's only a matter of time until the same dreary cycle repeats itself.

What really goes on in the pews when God's people gather together? How do people who sit in the pew behave in light of the fact that they are related to the Lord Jesus Christ, the head of the church?

Let's take a look at what Paul has to say about living and working in the church of Christ Jesus.

Building Bridges

My purpose is that they may be . . . united in love. Colossians 2:2

An American was telling a group of friends about a trip he'd recently taken to Africa. He'd gone there with a Christian relief organization to find and tap fresh water supplies for poor villages.

One day he and his African friends were traveling by Jeep from one village to another. They had journeyed a fair distance when they had to stop because a small bridge on their route had collapsed.

The American took one look at the problem and thought to himself, *No big deal. It should only take a couple of minutes to repair, and we can be on our way.*

Two Africans got out of the Jeep and inspected the broken bridge. Patiently they began discussing a possible remedy. This went on for ten minutes, then fifteen, then twenty, then half an hour. It was obvious the two did not agree on the best solution to the problem, and were quietly talking through the dilemma. The American, glancing at his watch, grew impatient.

For Pete's sake, guys, one of you just take charge and tell the other what to do, he thought. *We don't have time for all this!*

But the Africans continued their conversation, and only after coming to some sort of agreement did they get the bridge repaired. Once they went to work, the repairs took but a few minutes.

The American was steaming. He was about to lay into one of his African hosts when the man explained what had just taken place. Neither African had wanted to offend the other by insisting on his method of bridge first aid. Either method would have worked, and both would have taken about the same amount of time, but these men treasured friendship above time management. In their culture, maintaining good relationships was more important than maintaining schedules.

The American gulped.

Here I came to teach, he thought, *and I'm the one who's learning.*

Those African men knew that one of the best ways to encourage a brother is to be united in spirit with him. That's exactly what the apostle Paul taught the Colossian church, and it's a lesson we desperately need to learn. Paul wanted the church to be united in love.

What are some ways each Christian can contribute to the unity of the church?

Father, please help me to remember today that relationships are more important than programs in your scheme of things.

The Lone Ranger Should Join a Church

. . . united in love, so that they may have the full riches of complete understanding. Colossians 2:2

There is a very real sense in which we cannot grow spiritually in isolation. You can study, have devotions, and grow to a certain extent on your own—and you should—but there are many, many things you need to do corporately if you are to "have the full riches of complete understanding."

If you operate all on your own with the Lord Jesus, then you are limited in your understanding. If, on the other hand, you relate to the Lord Jesus in the fellowship of others, the discoveries they have made can benefit you, and your discoveries can enrich them. You'll begin to knock the rough edges off each other and encourage each other.

One of my favorite times of the week is Monday morning. I know that most pastors take Mondays off, but we don't. We gather early in the morning as a staff to study the Scriptures and discuss theology.

You know why it's one of my favorite times? It's because I know that the more I know, the more I know that I don't know. I'm so grateful for the gifted, godly men and women that God has gathered around me.

We knock the corners off each other. We make great theological pronouncements, and the others fall off their chairs laughing. What an encouragement this can be.

We are united in love in order that we might come to a full understanding.

How does this work for you? You need a spiritual environment in which you relate to others.

There is so much of God to know. There is so much in me to be changed. There is so much in the world to do. If I'm satisfied with knowing God minimally, allowing minimal change in my life, and making minimal impact on my world, then I am a living testimonial to my own shallowness.

But if I begin to think in terms of being united in love with others to have a fuller understanding of things, then I will make it a priority to be involved in the church.

Do you want to grow spiritually? Do you want to become more and more like Christ? Do you want the strength of character, depth of understanding, and gladness of spirit that only come with maturing faith?

Then make sure you're in a church environment where you are growing in unity with others.

God isn't looking for Lone Ranger Christians. The ones who try it look more like Lonely Ranger Christians to me. You don't need that, and neither do I.

So let's get involved! I need you, and you need me. That's what the church is all about.

Are you involved in a church or a small group where you are able to grow in your knowledge of God through your interaction and friendship with others?

> *Father, please help me to notice when I am beginning to become shallow in my relationship with you, and to take action to grow deeper in my understanding of you.*

Break Down the Barriers

Here there is no Greek or Jew, circumcised or uncircumcised, barbarian, Scythian, slave or free, but Christ is all, and is in all. Colossians 3:11

One of the most awesome major league baseball teams in history was the Oakland Athletics of the early 1970s. The team won three straight world championships, something no one else has done since.

You never would have guessed it had you visited their locker room.

They fought like cats and dogs. They needled each other, scuffled with each other, called each other names, played nasty tricks on each other.

But when they got out on the playing field, they were nearly unbeatable. Why?

Because when it came time for the game to begin, they put everything else aside and focused on baseball.

Paul has something very like that in mind here. He says the people in the pews are focused on Christ. They have all kinds of varying interests and ideas. But when they come together as believers, all those ideas are subjected to the one predominant idea—Christ is all that matters. He is the focus of our attention; he is the one we seek to honor, to love, and to serve.

Believers know that Christ dwells in them through the Holy Spirit. Whatever may be happening in their lives, they must see that he is alive in them and in others. It is the same Lord living and working in every believer. That is what binds them together.

Diverse interests, prejudices, and priorities in any group are bound to generate problems. If, however, these things become secondary, not primary, then the fellowship of believers will flourish.

Paul had to overcome all kinds of barriers in the church at Colosse: racial and ethnic differences, religious differences, cultural differences, social differences.

Occasionally I hear rumbles in my own church over social distinctions. Some groups make sure they never get together with other groups. It's hard for me to understand. I'd love to take these people by the hand and drop them in the church at Colosse, where they'd find both slaves and slave owners. Paul says when you focus on Christ, social distinctions don't count for much.

When we focus on Christ, all barriers are transcended. Lose your focus on Christ, and there will be as many barriers as people.

What is it that splits a church? It is people who major on differences. When our focus is on Christ—when he is allowed to work in each of our lives—then these barriers can be transcended in him.

Where is the focus in your church family? On Christ? Or on differences?

Father, please help us as a church to focus on you and learn to really love one another despite our differences.

God's Special People

Therefore, as God's chosen people, holy and dearly loved, clothe yourselves with compassion, kindness, humility, gentleness and patience. . . . And over all these virtues put on love, which binds them all together in perfect unity. Colossians 3:12-14

We are all accustomed to speaking of the Jews as God's chosen people. It's scriptural. But there's something especially fascinating about what Paul says concerning the church here. It's hidden just under the surface: ". . . God's chosen people, holy and dearly loved." All those expressions are picked straight out of Deuteronomy 7:6-8, where they apply to Israel.

The New Testament calls the church "the Israel of God" (Gal. 6:16). Many of the things that applied to Israel as a chosen people—holy and specially loved by God—now apply to the church. Why? Because just as God wanted a people, a community, which was readily identified with him in Old Testament days, so he wants a people, a community, which is readily identifiable with him now. That new community is the church.

Christians must understand that they are called to relate, not only to Christ, but to a community of believers. God doesn't just want individuals running around the place; he wants a clearly distinguishable, distinctive people—dearly loved, set apart, chosen to be his people. That is why an individual Christian should always be identified with a specific community of believers. We are not only to model our Christianity individually; we are to model it corporately as a people of God.

These people of God are to demonstrate unique behavior. Community behavior in the church is not like community behavior outside the church. Community behavior in the church is characterized by Christian graces. Paul says believers are to be "clothed" with them, which suggests the need to put out some effort. Notice the sorts of things that Christians are to be clothed with: "compassion, kindness, humility, gentleness and patience." These are nearly the same things listed in the "Fruit of the Spirit" passage in Galatians 5. Christian graces blossom in our lives as the Holy Spirit works in and through us and as we make an effort to cooperate with him.

Am I characterized by compassion and kindness, humility, gentleness, and patience? By nature I know I'm not. Enough people have told me so. And yet the Spirit of God is working on the old man.

Once in a while, do you get a glimmer of progress in this area? I profoundly hope so. I hope all of us can be honest and say, "Yes, I am lacking in compassion. I'm not very kind. I'm not very humble, either. I thought I was. I got all humble and then I got proud of it."

Maybe we can look at ourselves and say, "This is what I am, but by the grace of God changes are taking place. I'm working on it. I'm troubled and concerned about it. I want to be part of a community characterized by these things. I know it's going to take the work of the Spirit in my life and my cooperative effort with him."

What binds all these things together? What keeps them functioning as they ought? "Over all these virtues," writes Paul, "put on love, which binds them all together in perfect unity."

What does it mean to you to be called "God's chosen people, holy and dearly loved"?

> *Lord, thank you for giving me compassion, kindness, humility, gentleness, and patience to put on. Please help me to remember to clothe myself in them.*

Concrete Walls or Flexible Cables?

Bear with each other and forgive whatever grievances you may have against one another. Forgive as the Lord forgave you. Colossians 3:13

Isn't it easy to get fed up with God's people? The problem, quite frankly, is that the church of Jesus Christ is made up exclusively of redeemed sinners. And these wretched sinners—I'm one of them—have an awful habit of showing their true colors. If we're going to come down like a ton of bricks on everybody who shows his true colors, then there is going to be an awful pile of bricks around the place. It's amazing how far a little forbearance will go.

I'm not saying we turn a blind eye to things. I'm not saying we shrug our shoulders or let anything go. Christian grace isn't license. It's an attitude that begins to bind together the most disparate groups of people—different in race, social position, and education.

How on earth are you going to get people this dissimilar into one new community? You won't, unless there is Christian grace, Christian attitude, and Christian action.

Anybody who's been around the church for a while can talk about forgiveness. We've all heard so much about it. It's easy to shrug it aside. Recently I heard a new wrinkle on the idea that renewed my appreciation for what it involves.

It came from a TV program about stock car drivers. You say, "That will be real helpful on forgiveness, I'm sure." Well, it was. As a group sat in class learning how to be stock car drivers, the lecturer said that the first thing to remember about stock car racing was this: Concrete walls are very unforgiving.

Unforgiving people remind you of concrete walls. You've got a bit of momentum in your life, you've gone off track a little, you're heading for trouble—but fortunately, somebody has put a concrete wall in your way. *Kaboom!* And that solves everything.

No, it doesn't. It just makes things ten times worse.

One day I would like to go up in a fighter plane and land on the deck of an aircraft carrier in a rough sea.

Just imagine coming in on one of those fighters. You see the aircraft carrier down below, its flight deck the size of a postage stamp. "I sure hope they know what they're doing," you say. You swoop down at two hundred miles per hour, and as you hit the flight deck, you discover, unfortunately, that someone's built a concrete wall across your path. *Kaboom!* As you splatter yourself on the windshield, you moan, "Well, at least I'm not in the ocean."

No, they don't build concrete walls across flight decks. They string a cable across, designed to catch a hook on the underside of the plane. The cable has all kinds of give in it. It takes the steam out of the plane's speed and brings it to a halt.

The difference between forgiving and unforgiving is the difference between concrete walls and flexible cable. Forgiving is necessary in the fellowship of believers all the time, because there is always somebody upset with somebody. There's always some evangelical nose out of joint somewhere. And the last thing that bent evangelical noses need is to be smashed into concrete walls.

Is there someone in your life who needs your forgiveness?

Father, thank you for your forgiveness—for your example and enablement.

A Peaceful, Grateful Heart

Let the peace of Christ rule in your hearts, since as members of one body you were called to peace. And be thankful. Colossians 3:15

I wish I never heard conversations like the following, but I'm afraid they occur all the time:

"I'm going to do such and such a thing, even though some people tell me it's wrong."

"How can you do that?"

"I've got peace about it."

"Doesn't the fact that God tells you not to do it mean anything?"

"I've got peace about it."

"But Scripture says it's wrong."

"I don't care. I've got peace about it."

These confused people nullify an objective truth by their subjective experience of peace. Now, it's true that Paul says we are to be governed by peace: "Let the peace of Christ rule in your hearts." He did not, however, mean "peace" as an individual, personal, subjective thing.

The problem is that subjective "peace" can be nothing more than the chloroforming of the conscience. Give your conscience a hard time long enough, tell it "phooey" long enough, and in the end your conscience will tell you to go ahead and live as you please. You can call that "peace" if you want to, but that's not what Paul's writing about here.

When Paul mentions "peace," he is talking about a sense of order in relationships between Christians. Believers are called to orderly behavior. We are not called to hassling, fighting, or arguing. We are not called to cliques, schisms, or feuds. We in the church are to be governed by peace.

This peace, Paul says, is to have a traveling buddy named "thankfulness." One evening our church had a great quarterly meeting of pastors, elders, and deacons. The last hour was devoted to people standing up and declaring one thing for which they were thankful, one new thing they had seen God do in our fellowship during the previous year. We had to cut it off after an hour. You walk out on air after a meeting like that.

It's amazing what a dash of thankfulness will do. It's amazing what a commitment to peace and order in the fellowship will do. It begins to produce the body of Christ.

What does Paul mean when he talks about the peace of Christ?

Lord, I want Christ's peace to rule in my relationships with others. Please help me to be thankful, too, regardless of the circumstances.

What Matters Most

Let the word of Christ dwell in you richly as you teach and admonish one another with all wisdom, and as you sing psalms, hymns and spiritual songs with gratitude in your hearts to God. Colossians 3:16

When you pick a church to join (horrible thought that we do it that way, but let's accept it), make absolutely certain you know its priorities. Is it a community of believers that holds high the Word of Christ? Is it committed to allowing that Word to dwell richly within it and among it? Find a church that deviates from the Word, and you've found a church on the way out.

Praise is another element which ought constantly to enrich the community of believers. The fellowship of believers is a praising community, where people who can sing beautifully, sing beautifully; and those who just sing, just sing; and those who have voices like crows with laryngitis croak to the glory of God. But nobody just sits there like an old sourpuss, looking as if they had lost their last friend, having had their breakfast of onions.

Some have tried to differentiate between "psalms" and "hymns" and "spiritual songs," but I think such distinctions are more a work of creativity than of fact. We know that the Lord Jesus and his disciples, after the first Communion, sang a hymn and went out to the Mount of Olives. And we know exactly what they would sing at that particular time—it would be Psalms 115, 116, 117, and 118. The "hymns" they sang were psalms.

We also know what songs will be sung in heaven, because Revelation tells us. "They sang a new song," it says, and even gives the lyrics. At other times when we read the word *hymn* in our English Bibles, it's actually from the Greek word for "psalm."

Still, Paul gives us one interesting insight into this issue from 1 Corinthians 14. In that letter he told the Corinthians that when they came together, some would have a word, some would have a hymn, some would have a prophecy, and some would have a tongue. Small groups of Corinthians got together, and in the free-flowing worship time that ensued, someone might step forward and announce, "I wrote a hymn. I'd like to sing it." And so they would all sing the hymn.

It would take a long time for churches with thousands of attenders to invite everyone to come up to the platform one after another and sing the hymns they'd written that week. That's the idea in this passage, though. It's an invitation for everyone to get involved.

"Oh, I couldn't write a hymn!"

You couldn't? Have you ever tried?

"Oh, I couldn't write a song!"

You couldn't? Have you ever tried?

"I could never sing!"

You couldn't? Have you ever tried?

Listen, the community of believers is a praising community. It is a group of people, rooted in the psalms and in the Scriptures, who love to join together to sing God's praises with a heart of gratitude. Enrichment is the natural result.

In your life and in your church, how important is praising him through music? How can the Word of God "dwell in you richly"?

Father, thank you for the gift of your Word, for the gift of music, and for how these gifts help us to worship you.

Meditations on Life in the Pew

1. Read prayerfully through Acts 2:42-47, thinking about what made the early church grow so rapidly, and praying that the Lord would help you think of how we today might imitate its practices.

2. What does 1 Corinthians 12:12-31 say about what it means to work together as the body of Christ?

3. Read Ephesians 2:11-22 out loud, slowly, a few times. What does it mean when it says that "he himself is our peace" (v. 14)?

4. Write down Hebrews 10:24-25 on an index card and tape it up on your dashboard, on your wall at work, or on your refrigerator—somewhere you can see it often as you think of ways to carry it out.

5. As you read through 1 Peter 2:4-12, think about what Peter states is one of the purposes of the church.

How Does My Family Fit In?

Families today are in deep trouble. Even Christian families. When relationships sour and marriages get shaky, all too often Christian people do exactly what we expect of unbelievers. They split, divide up everything, divvy up the care of the children, and head in different directions.

This is deeply troubling, because clearly it is not an adequate response to a dreadful problem. If you as a believer are having tensions in your marriage or your family, don't look first of all for secular advice or secular solutions. Assume there's a good chance that underlying your marital or family problems are some major spiritual problems, and that if those spiritual difficulties can be ironed out, your family problems may well take care of themselves.

Do not misunderstand; this is no rap against marriage and family counseling. Neither is it a rap against Christian counseling. I totally support what professionals in those fields are doing. They're vital to helping solve many of the problems we confront.

But I am convinced that many, many marriage and family problems are really problems of disobedience. And the only solution is down-to-earth, gutsy obedience, lived out in the power of the Holy Spirit.

If that were not true, why would the apostle Paul put this practical teaching on family living in the context of profound theological and spiritual truth?

There's something else we need to notice, too. Have you ever enjoyed a concert by the world-famous one-armed violinist? Probably not—there isn't one. One-armed people can't play the violin.

Have you ever been out on a lovely afternoon in the wilderness, looked up into the sky, and seen circling there, effortlessly up in the air currents, a gorgeous, one-winged eagle? Probably not. One-winged eagles can't fly.

When you look into Colossians 3:18-21, at first sight you will see four points. Verse 18 speaks to wives, verse 19 to husbands, verse 20 to children, and verse 21 to fathers.

There are two couplets of truth here. The first relates to husbands and wives; the second, to parents and children. Never try teaching wives to submit to their husbands apart from admonishing husbands to love their wives. And by the same token, don't try teaching children to obey their parents apart from reminding parents not to embitter their children. The two come together like the arms of a violinist, like the wings of an eagle.

Ladies First

Wives, submit to your husbands, as is fitting in the Lord.
Colossians 3:18

If you want to antagonize a lot of women today, just tell them the apostle Paul is a friend of yours. Prepare to be assaulted. Paul does not do well in feminist circles.

A lot of women today aren't into submission.

But neither are men. In fact, most people aren't into submission. Many positively despise it. But submission is a normal human experience. Without it society cannot survive.

Although God is the one in whom all authority resides, the Scriptures tell us he delegates some of it to human authorities in order that society might flourish. For that delegated authority to function, submission must take place—and, if necessary, be enforced. When submission to authority breaks down, society comes apart at the seams.

But submission is more than that. It is a particularly Christian attitude. A Christian is a person who acknowledges Jesus Christ as Lord; that's the essence of Christianity. As soon as you say, "Lord," you assume submission.

This strikes at the heart of why many people are not interested in Christianity. It's not that they would not like many of its benefits—they'd be terrifically interested in those. But they refuse to submit to the lordship of Christ.

They won't very often admit that's the reason. In fact, they'll come up with all kinds of arguments, debates, and discussions to claim otherwise. But the underlying reason they reject Christianity is its demands for them to relate to Jesus Christ on the basis of his lordship.

"Why do you call me 'Lord, Lord,'" Jesus asked on one occasion, "and do not do the things that I say?" It is utter nonsense to live in disobedience to Jesus while still calling him Lord. The essence of relating to lordship is submissive obedience. And that is the basis upon which Paul gives instructions to husbands and wives.

It's in the context of this theme of obedience that the apostle, in the book of Ephesians, introduces the idea of wives submitting to their husbands. In Ephesians 5:21-22 Paul wrote, "Submit to one another out of reverence for Christ. Wives, submit to your husbands as to the Lord." It is in that setting that we teach the wife to submit to her husband.

Notice, too, that the idea of the wife's submitting to her husband in Ephesians 5 is a result of Paul's statement that, in the same way that Christ is the head of the church, the husband is the head of the wife.

As soon as we say "head," we unfortunately think in terms of "head honcho." That is precisely what gets some women upset about submitting to their husbands. They've got this image of the "head honcho" standing up there immovable, infallible, unapproachable, and unbearable . . . and they're supposed to submit to him?

But this is a total caricature of what Paul says. Paul is not thinking merely in terms of leadership and response to leadership—though that idea is clearly there—but of leadership that is deeply concerned to strengthen the relationship, nourishing, cherishing, and helping the other to mature.

Assuming the husband understands biblical headship, it will not be too difficult for a wife to say, "You know, it's pretty obvious that somebody has to be the leader here. This leadership is the resource from which I'm drawing help and encouragement all the time. Therefore it's pointless to buck it or to fight it. I'll join in and live in the good of it."

Paul says submission of wives to husbands is "fitting," or appropriate. Why? Because submissive attitudes on everyone's part are essential for society's well-being, and because submission on the part of every Christian clearly demonstrates to the world the lordship of Christ.

Do you think of submission as primarily positive or negative? Why?

Heavenly Father, please help me to submit to Christ's lordship in my life, and to have a better attitude about submitting to the authorities you have put over me here on earth.

Big Man and the Little Woman

Husbands, love your wives and do not be harsh with them.
Colossians 3:19

Colossian women were accustomed to submission. Their culture required it. When Paul said, "Wives, submit to your husbands," they no doubt responded, "So what's new? Wives around here have always had to submit to their husbands. We're just pieces of property—chattel. We don't have any other option but to submit."

But then Paul turned to the husbands. "Husbands, love your wives," he commanded.

It doesn't look radical at all to us. But to the men of first-century Colosse, it was one of the most radical statements they had ever heard. "You've got to be kidding," they sputtered. "We don't have to love our wives! You don't love chattel." Husbands weren't even remotely interested in loving their wives. It just wasn't done.

Before I get after the men too much about loving their wives, let's remind ourselves that love makes the world go 'round. Psychologists tell us that the most common problem of those with aberrant psychological behavior is their inability to express or to receive love. These unhappy people "short circuit" from lack of love. All human beings are made to love to be loved.

In Ephesians 5:25-29, Paul describes Christ's love for the church as a model of how a husband ought to love his wife. Christ loved the church so much he gave himself up for her.

Everybody is good at being selfish, but perhaps men are better at it than women. It demonstrates love when a man—an innately insensitive, selfish creature—begins to unselfishly give up himself for his wife.

Perhaps it's at this point that some of us are having problems. We don't need a lot of ongoing therapy. What we need is men who will unselfishly give up themselves for their wives.

Christ also cares for the church and feeds her. One of the legitimate raps on men by women goes something like this: "He doesn't care what I think or how I feel. He's out there doing his own thing. He comes back in when he's good and ready, sits down in front of the tube, puts up his feet, and demands, 'Where's my shirt for tomorrow morning?' Then he tells me to keep the kids quiet. I'm glad he's here, but I wish he'd get off my case!"

I wonder what would happen if a husband started to care enough about her to be interested in what she thinks and feels. When a husband understands what his wife is saying, feeling, and thinking, then responds to it, accepting his responsibility to nourish and encourage her in that area—that's when real spirituality breaks out and grows.

How do you do this? Paul says you do it by regarding her as you would your own body. In the same way that Christ looks at the church as his body, the husband looks at his wife as part of himself. If husbands would do this, good marriages would blossom and flourish all over the country.

When wives submit to their husbands and husbands love their wives, we're going to get a balance. There'll be no one-armed violinists, no one-winged eagles.

But what if your spouse is a wretch? What if your spouse sniffs at Paul's words to husbands and wives? What if . . .

Instead of talking about all the exceptions, let's start with ourselves and respond to God's working in our hearts by his Spirit.

Is there a problem in your family that could be cured with a little submission and love?

Father, please help submission and love to more and more characterize my Christian walk, my life in general, and my interactions with people in my family.

Chips Off the Old Block

Children, obey your parents in everything, for this pleases the Lord.
Colossians 3:20

I remember a time when our eldest child was about one year old. He was staggering around the kitchen, holding on to things to keep himself afloat.

Three racks filled with vegetables sat in one corner, the top rack loaded with ripe tomatoes. I saw him stumble over toward these delicacies and inspect them. A smile crept over his face as he picked up one to look closer. Soon it was no longer in his hand. *Splash!* It was now on the wall.

"David, do not do that!" I commanded.

He looked at me, all twelve months of him, and picked up a second one.

"Do not do it, do not do it," I repeated.

Splash!

I grabbed his little hand and said, "Don't do it! What you've done is worthy of corporal punishment. You do it again and you'll get some sergeant punishment."

He picked up the next one.

"Don't do it, David, don't you do it. I'll spank you if you do."

Splash!

We were getting low on tomatoes by this time. He therefore decided a slight change of tactics was in order. He picked up the fourth tomato, held his other little hand out, and said, "Spank it, Daddy." Then he was ready.

Splash!

I picked him up and announced, "You're going to your room, David." I took him there, stood him on a little chest that made him the same height as I, and gave him a little talking to with my preacher's finger. As my finger came forward the third time, he caught it, stuck it in his mouth, and bit.

At the same time my wife walked in.

"Admit it, you're beaten," she advised.

She was right, unfortunately.

You know, it's hard to teach your kids obedience. That's why we simply give up on it so often . . . and why we produce so many little sociopaths. Our society is marked by lack of respect for authority. School teachers complain about it all the time, and they're quitting by the busloads. What a tragedy! Sunday school teachers have had it with these kids, and youth workers complain it's the hardest thing in the world to get these kids to do what they're supposed to do.

What's the problem? The problem is back home!

Bill Cosby explains it in his own inimitable way: "Parents don't want justice; they just want peace and quiet."

He's right.

Rather than dealing with children in a way that firmly yet gently leads them along, we give up. Kids don't bother about being obedient, and ironically, their parents end up embittering and discouraging them.

Why is it so important to teach children to obey?

Father, please help me to be a good example to the children who watch me—by obeying you and the authorities you've placed over me.

Two Wings

Fathers, do not embitter your children, or they will become discouraged. Colossians 3:21

We observed "two wings" when we talked abut husbands and wives, and we see "two wings" again when Paul gives instructions to parents and children. Here is the parents' side. The word for *fathers* here is the same word found in Hebrews 11:23 and can also mean *parents*. For the sake of convenience in this general context, let's assume it is parents.

"Do what I say."

"Why?"

"Because I said so."

That's one approach, and it's sometimes valid—particularly when the parent doesn't know why: "I don't know why, but my parents made me do it, so it's your turn now. You can get even later."

Telling someone to obey, like telling someone to submit, often prompts a reaction. And yet obedience is a normal human experience, just like submission. Sooner or later you'll learn it. April 15 you'll learn it. Drive down the freeway in full view of a little sign that says 55, ignore it, multiply it by two, and keep going—you'll learn it. Everybody learns obedience.

Somebody has said, "Man was made with a will; little boys were made with a won't." That's probably true. That's how you discover you've got a will, by exercising your "won't." Everyone who has a will has a won't, and whether you will or you won't determines the quality of life you'll enjoy.

Christians understand this and have made their decision. Just as the Lord Jesus Christ said to his Father, "Not my will, but thine be done," the Christian has said to the Lord Jesus, "Not my will, but thine be done."

Christians are people who are uniquely committed to being obedient. That being the case, parents have a special responsibility to the little rascals they bring into the world. It's their job to equip their children to become healthy members of society and mature believers in the Lord, to fit them for earth and for eternity.

You'll never fit them for earth or for heaven unless you teach them obedience. They have to learn it. Life without discipline is chaos, and discipline has to be learned the hard way.

Unfortunately, many parents have the wrong idea about discipline. They are either unbending in it or negligent with it, and they wind up embittering their children. Paul cautions us against that.

There are two equally effective ways of embittering your children. You can embitter them by being too strict and by not giving them the freedom to develop. Or you can embitter them by giving so much freedom that they get the feeling you couldn't care less what happens to them. Both methods work equally well.

It seems to me that the best preventative and antidote to those bad attitudes is to remember the Lord, the one to whom those children really belong. True, you brought them into the world, but he expects you to work to fit them for earth and for heaven.

This is going to take an awful lot of diligence and perseverance on your part, a lot of obedience on your children's part, and all the resources of which Colossians speaks. There are no shortcuts.

Parents and children—get the two wings flapping. If you want a smooth flight, it's the only way.

How can you avoid irritating and discouraging those you are responsible to discipline?

Father, when it is necessary for me to help others learn obedience, please help me to balance love and authority in a way that reflects your way with your children.

Meditations on Life in the Family

1. Read thoughtfully through Deuteronomy 6. How important is it to talk frequently with your children about the things of God?

2. What specific things does Solomon advise his son about in Proverbs 1:8-19; 2:1-11; and 3:1-12? What do you think of these as topics for discussion in your family?

3. How does 1 Corinthians 7:3-5 remind you of the one-winged eagle or the one-armed violinist?

4. Read slowly through Ephesians 5:22–6:4, thinking about how marriage is like Christ's relationship to the church.

5. Read through 1 Peter 3:1-7, then turn back to Genesis chapters 16 and 21. As you return to 1 Peter and look through it again, think about what submission means. Does Sarah's "submission" mean she had no mind of her own?

What about Work?

You can almost hear the seven dwarves singing as you read the bumper sticker on the car in front of you: "I owe, I owe, so off to work I go!"

Almost. Somewhere along the way, somebody changed the words to the song. And not only the words—they changed the sentiment, too.

Do you remember Disney's version of Snow White and the Seven Dwarfs? The dwarfs were a happy, contented bunch (Grumpy excepted), glad for the opportunity to work. They didn't complain about it (Grumpy excepted)—they whistled while they worked. They worked because they liked to work. Their song was, "Hi ho, hi ho, it's off to work we go!" and they sang it with delight.

Enter the bumper sticker. Gone is the idea of work as joy. Today people work to pay bills. If they didn't have to pay bills, they wouldn't work. Work isn't a joy for them, it's a curse.

If people whistled while they worked in our society, their coworkers would question either their manners ("Ugh! Why doesn't he cut that out?"), their morals ("Hmmm. I wonder what he's up to?"), or their mind ("Yikes! A wacko that likes to work!").

We'd think something was out of kilter somewhere. The truth is, something is out of kilter—but what's fouled up is our negative view of work. It turns out the dwarfs are closer to Paul's teaching on work than many of us are.

Paul sees work as a gift of God. He sees it as an opportunity to revel in God's provision and grace. He wants us to do it gladly, delightedly, as to God himself. He doesn't want us to weasel out as much pay for as little work as possible.

So let's work for him heartily, gladly, with gusto. Nobody pays better, and the benefits are out of this world. Literally.

Off to Work We Go

Slaves, obey your earthly masters in everything; and do it, not only when their eye is on you and to win their favor, but with sincerity of heart and reverence for the Lord. . . . Masters, provide your slaves with what is right and fair. Colossians 3:22; 4:1

What is the best way to please your boss? By doing your work, and doing it well. There is nothing new about this. In fact, there is an old saying—not quite as old as the Bible, but better known—which says, "An honest day's pay for an honest day's work." It's a good, old-fashioned idea, and it's thoroughly biblical.

What is the best way to get employees to do what you want them to? It is by looking after them, caring for them, showing that you are interested in them as people, encouraging, helping, and developing them. The best way to ensure that your workers do well for you is to provide for them what is right and fair.

That's the Bible's idea of mutuality.

Unfortunately, this idea is often turned inside-out. It becomes, "How much can I get out of that fat cat, and how little do I need to do for him?" on one side, and "How little do I need to give that guy in order to squeeze the last drop of production out of him?" on the other.

How far removed this is from biblical teaching!

This idea of doing what is right and good extends to methods of working. Notice the expression "not only when their eye is on you." The Greek word here is one that Paul perhaps made up himself. Translated literally, it means "eye service." If you are an employer, do you feel that you need to keep your eye on people all the time? Or do you know, whether you are there or not, that you can count on your employees to be thoroughly reliable?

If you are employing Christians, you have every right to expect them to produce whether you are there or not. And if you are a believer, you ought to expect to work as hard whether you're being watched or not.

Most people today consider this strange thinking. It's different from the norm. But it's thoroughly Christian.

In one factory, a suggestion box was installed for people to contribute ideas designed to improve working conditions. The first suggestion requested that the foreman no longer wear rubber heels on his shoes. They wanted to hear him coming.

That well-known theologian, Groucho Marx, said, "No man leaves before his time—unless, of course, the boss has gone home early."

The common attitude today is to do one standard of work if your boss is watching, and another if he isn't. Paul specifically addresses this, and says Christians are not to do the minimum required to keep the boss happy.

Christians believe work is a gift from God. We do not get our theology from the Fall, where work is seen as onerous and a curse. We get our theology from Creation, where we see that God himself worked, and that we were created to work.

We see God incarnate in the person of Christ, working in Nazareth. We recognize that God has given us skills, time, and energy, and that if we are to be fulfilled and truly glorify God, we will use these skills, our time, and our energy well.

We see work as a gracious calling, and we do it with joy.

Work equals joy. Does it seem like a strange equation to you? Then perhaps it's time you brushed up on the mathematical tables of heaven. Ask the teacher, Jesus, for some help. I'm sure he'll be glad to assist you.

I'm also sure he'll give you some homework.

If you were to be constantly aware that you are working for the Lord, are there any work styles or habits that would change?

Father, please help me to see my work as more of a joy and a gift from you. Help me to see work in general as a blessing, not a curse.

Thank God—It's Monday!

Slaves, obey your earthly masters . . . with sincerity of heart and reverence for the Lord. Whatever you do, work at it with all your heart, as working for the Lord, not for men, since you know that you will receive an inheritance from the Lord as a reward. It is the Lord Christ you are serving. Colossians 3:22-24

A young woman in our church told me that when she arrives in the morning to teach her Sunday school class, she tries to think of the Lord Jesus Christ sitting there in the back row. It completely changes her attitude to her lesson and toward her kids.

This is exactly what Paul has in mind here. He says the proper motivation for work is not material gain, but something deeply spiritual.

Christians are to work wholeheartedly. Whatever you do, he says, work at it with all your heart, and with eternal things in mind. Not just because it's right (although it is), but because there will be a reward.

I was talking to a group of pastors one day about all the problems and frustrations of the pastorate. One of them said, "In the end, they can't pay you enough for this job. The only reason anybody would ever do it would be out of a sense of calling."

I'd like to think this was true of every Christian, that at work we are putting out so prodigiously that they couldn't pay us enough for it—and that we are there because of a sense of calling.

Have you ever thought about your job in that way? When you get up in the morning to brush your teeth and get ready for work, do you think, "Wow, God has called me to this job. I wonder what he'll ask me to do today?"

A job is not just a job. God has put you where he has for reasons that he may not reveal, but for reasons that please him. As long as he keeps you there, make sure that you honor his call. When you do, you'll not only become a valuable showpiece of God's grace in your workplace, but you'll experience the peace and contentment that God showers on those who honor him. That's a call to get excited about!

Those who want to develop such an excitement about their call need to add one more thing to their portfolio, Paul says. Twice in Colossians 3:22–4:1 Paul speaks of what his readers already know. "You know that you will receive an inheritance from the Lord . . . you know that you have a Master in heaven." In back of their work habits is good theology.

Paul's readers needed to understand who Christ is and how they were related to him. The apostle was convinced that a thorough knowledge of these things would get them excited about what it meant to serve Christ.

Whether they were at church, in the family, or at work, Paul says if they took to heart the words of God they would be distinctive people.

Nothing has changed since then.

One of the great places where we get the chance to live out our Christianity is at work.

Does knowing that believers will "receive an inheritance from the Lord" motivate you to work hard? Why or why not?

Father, whatever I do, I want to do it for you and remember that you have called me to do it, for your own reasons. Help me to trust you and to remember to do it wholeheartedly and joyfully, to please you.

The Master's Voice

Slaves, obey your earthly masters in everything; and do it . . . with . . . reverence for the Lord. Whatever you do, work at it with all your heart, as working for the Lord, not for men. . . . It is the Lord Christ you are serving. . . . Masters, provide your slaves with what is right and fair, because you know that you also have a Master in heaven. Colossians 3:22-24; 4:1

I want you to notice something that is slightly below the surface of this passage. The Greek word for *Lord, Kyrios,* can also be translated *master.* Paul riddled this passage of Scripture with the word *kyrios* in order to make a play on the words *Lord* and *master.* Read through Colossians 3:22–4:1 in your Bible, using the Greek word *kyrios* wherever you see the words *master* or *Lord.*

Do you see the dominant theme of Paul's message? The dominant theme is lordship.

What makes all the difference to believers everywhere is that Jesus Christ is their Lord.

For Paul's day, this teaching was radical in the extreme.

It's not a great deal less radical today. When we find ourselves in difficult circumstances in the workplace, our normal response is to try to change the circumstances.

But Paul says when Christians find themselves in difficult circumstances, they don't immediately change their circumstances. They change their attitude.

When I get up on a Monday morning and get in the car to drive to work, what is my mental attitude?

If I am an employee, my reaction to those in authority over me will demonstrate my attitude to authority in general, and particularly as it is delegated from the ultimate authority, the Lord Jesus.

If I am an employer, I always bear in mind that as I exercise authority over my employees, I have one in authority over me—the Lord Jesus.

Whether I am an employer or an employee, I must remember that I serve the Lord Christ.

The RCA company used to have as its trade symbol a dog staring at a phonograph, accompanied by the words, "His master's voice." I never saw the dog do a thing but sit there, but from the way he was sitting I'll bet anything he'd jump if his master's voice said, "Jump!"

In Colossians 3:22–4:1, our Master, the Lord Jesus, is telling us to jump—not out of fear or mere duty, but because he rewards faithful service.

Remember that the next time you go to work, and chances are that soon you'll be looking at your job in a whole new way. Your circumstances may not change, but you will—and you'll have one mighty pleased Lord in heaven.

How does your attitude about work demonstrate the fact that you are serving the Lord Jesus in all you do?

Father, please help my attitude at work to honor you in every way.

Meditations on Our Vocation

1. What two reasons do Proverbs 10:4-5 give for working hard at your job?

2. Copy 1 Thessalonians 4:11-12 on a three-by-five card and put it up on the dashboard of your car, inside your briefcase, or somewhere you will see it before work or on your way to work. What does this passage say about the effect of a good work ethic?

3. Read through 2 Thessalonians 3:6-15, thinking about why it is important to be diligent in our work.

4. What does 1 Timothy 6:1-2 imply about the relationship between a believing employee and a Christian employer?

5. What does James 5:1-6 say about the danger of success? How should successful Christian businesspeople treat their employees?

How Can I Get Involved?

Many years ago racial strife erupted in Boston over court-ordered school busing. The Boston Marathon was scheduled to take place while this strife was at its peak, and authorities considered canceling the race because part of the course ran through one of the city's most troubled areas. At last they decided to hold it as scheduled in the hope that it might bring people together.

One part of the course features a tortuous stretch known as Heartbreak Hill. Sadists that we are, that's where thousands of spectators gather. They love to see people struggling against the Heartbreak Hill. They stand and yell and shout as they see the heaving chests of weary runners about to collapse.

"Come on, 769, you can make it!"

"What's the matter with you? Don't let that old fellow beat you there!"

Now, most of the people shouting are fifty-five pounds overweight and probably couldn't run up a bill, let alone Heartbreak Hill. But that doesn't stop them from "encouraging."

On this day one young man had "hit the wall" as he approached the foot of Heartbreak Hill. It was highly doubtful he could go a step further. Spectators were shouting at him, "Come on, man, you can make it!" It wasn't helping at all.

In the middle of all this an older man, who was obviously in better shape than the younger runner, came alongside, put his arm around him, put his hip under the young man's hip, and spoke quietly to him. Together, step by step, slowly, painstakingly, they made their way up Heartbreak Hill.

The poignant thing about it was that the young man was black and the older man was white. What a powerful illustration of how to handle racial strife! Just get together, start to carry the burden of another, and encourage each other.

Encouragement is one of the most significant and important ministries, and you don't have to be particularly gifted to be an encourager. Anyone can encourage someone else. But too often this ministry is the one in which we involve ourselves the least. I don't know anybody who couldn't encourage, and I don't know anyone who couldn't use some encouragement.

The Greek word Paul uses for "encourage," *parakaleo,* is made up of two words. *Para* means "alongside." A paramedic is someone who works alongside a medical person. A parachurch organization works alongside a local church. *Kaleo* means "to call." The idea in the Greek, then, is "to call alongside."

Come alongside someone today! You can't provide any better or more valuable medicine anywhere on earth. And all it costs is your time.

Little Guys, Too!

You learned it from Epaphras, our dear fellow servant, who is a faithful minister of Christ on our behalf. Colossians 1:7

Notice that no one gets the message without a messenger. Paul says he delivered the message of God's grace to the Colossians, but as far as we know, he never even visited the city. How did he pull it off?

When he was in Ephesus, he discovered that a Greek teacher named Tyrannus had a school. Tyrannus didn't have classes in the middle of the day because it was too hot. Everybody took a siesta (or the Greek equivalent) in the afternoon, so Paul went to Tyrannus and said, "Could I borrow your schoolroom in the heat of the day?"

"Sure, for all the good it'll do you."

So Paul got his classroom, and he told the believers in Ephesus, "I'm going to teach theology in the heat of the day, when everybody else is in the sack. You guys get yourselves out of the sack and come here."

People came, and every day for two solid years Paul taught in the school of Tyrannus. Acts 19:10 tells us the most remarkable thing about these classes. Their influence wasn't restricted to Ephesus: "All the Jews and Greeks who lived in the province of Asia heard the word of the Lord."

The Asia it talks about isn't the continent we think of today. It was the Roman province of Asia, where Colosse, Hierapolis, Laodicea, Phrygia, Troas, and many other cities were to be found.

Because Paul taught for two years in Ephesus, every single one of these cities heard the word of the Lord—even though Paul never visited any of them. How did it work?

Sitting in class was a little fellow named Epaphras. You wouldn't notice him, just an ordinary little guy. Not an apostle or anything like that. He hadn't been to seminary, hadn't gone to Bible school, didn't have "Reverend" in front of his name.

But he sat down in class, taking it all in. Then one day Paul said, "Okay, folks, now this is what I want you to do. Everything you've learned, go tell somebody else."

Epaphras put up his hand and said, "Where should I start?"

"Well, where do you live?" Paul asked.

"Colosse," Epaphras replied.

"Start there," Paul said, so off Epaphras went to Colosse. He began with people he knew and started to share what he knew—from the human level. From the divine point of view, the gospel of the grace of God in all its truth was coming to Colosse.

When people like Paul and Epaphras go wherever God sends them, knowing what they believe, sharing what they believe, and demonstrating the reality of it in their lives, God works and brings people to faith in Christ.

Where do you think would be a good place for you to start?

Dear Father, please help my life to be a living demonstration of the reality of your grace and truth, and please give me the courage to share it verbally.

Pray and Tell

I want you to know how much I am struggling for you and for those at Laodicea, and for all who have not met me personally. Colossians 2:1

The word *struggling* comes from the arena. It's the word the Greeks used for wrestling. That's how concerned Paul was for these people—he "wrestled" for them.

I'll bet he's talking about prayer. That's how he could wrestle and agonize for somebody who was hundreds of miles away.

Every believer can show an interest in others by praying for them, then letting them know.

It's one thing to pray for people you know. It's another thing to exert yourself for those you've never met. It's doubtful that Paul ever visited the church at Colosse, but that didn't stop him from having a tremendous concern for them and taking time to pray earnestly for them.

Even though Paul was separated from the Colossians by hundreds of miles, he wanted to encourage them by expressing his concern for them.

It's possible for Christians to be so wrapped up in their own concerns that they show little care for anyone else. They ignore people outside their immediate universe.

Christian missionaries today are spread out over the face of the whole earth. They have sensed God's call to go hundreds and thousands of miles away from their homelands, to people whom they have never met. They are not willing to stand on the sidelines and say, "Come on, you guys in Ethiopia, you can make it!" They have gone alongside them, put their arms around them, and are going with them on the way.

God calls some of us to go abroad, but that doesn't mean the rest of us can stand on the sidelines. All of us should find at least one way to express concern for those we've never met, to encourage people whose faces we have never seen.

God doesn't want everybody to go overseas. But he would like everybody to struggle in prayer for other areas of the body of Christ.

The contact you have with them could be a note, a call, or a letter—anything that expresses your concern for them and reminds them that you are praying for them.

Paul went out of his way to let the Colossians know about his concern. He could have prayed and not said anything, but he starts off the chapter by saying, "I want you to know how much I am struggling for you."

I've often sat down and talked with missionaries, many of them in very lonely places. They often tell me how much it means to them to have regular contact with people they have never met who are genuinely concerned for them!

So when I get a prayer letter, I don't just look at it and trash it. I read it, pray immediately about it, underline something in it, and write a brief note to them. If you have never had contact with, concern for, and communication with someone you have never seen, think seriously about why you haven't. If you recognize that you probably should, take steps now—even little steps—to rectify it so that you, too, can be an encouragement to someone else.

Who are some people you could encourage through prayer and/or letters?

Father, please bring to my attention some faraway people you would like me to pray for and encourage, and help me to be faithful to support them as you would like me to.

An Ounce of Encouragement

My purpose is that they may be encouraged in heart. Colossians 2:2

Howard Hendricks says he owes his ministry to people who encouraged him.

He came from a poor home, where his parents had split up before he was born. On his first day in fifth grade, his teacher said, "Oh—Howard Hendricks. I've heard a lot about you. I understand you're the worst kid in this school." Challenged like that, Hendricks made sure she was right. Before the year was up he'd been gagged, tied to his chair, and punished in countless other ways.

When the next school year rolled around, Hendricks wasn't surprised when his sixth grade teacher said to him, "So you're Howard Hendricks. I've heard you're the worst boy in this school."

Hendricks thought, *Here we go again.*

But then she continued: "And you know what? I don't believe a word of it."

Throughout the next year she did everything she could to encourage the boy. She praised his work. She helped him when needed. She believed in him. And Hendricks credits her with changing his life forever.

That's what encouragement can do.

Paul knew that if you take the time to encourage people, you can give them new strength, new desire. And nothing encourages people more than to be commended for something well done.

If the church really is the body of Christ, then one part of the body cannot say to the other, "I don't need you." How wonderful it would be if the church in America were so alert to current events, so interested and concerned, that it would communicate with its brothers all over the world, struggle with them, and encourage them in prayer.

I can't imagine that there is one single believer anywhere who could not be involved in that kind of ministry. And I know there is not one single believer anywhere who would not be encouraged by such a ministry.

With that much need and that much opportunity, let's get started right away!

Who do you know who is working hard for the Lord, who would be encouraged by some commendation and inspiration?

Father, please help me to be aware of those around me and of world events so that I can be honest, realistic, and accurate in my encouragement of and prayers for others.

Keep Looking Up

Devote yourselves to prayer. Colossians 4:2

Many children are convinced that adults give orders solely for the sake of giving orders.

"Do the dishes, won't you, honey?" Mom asks.

Why? the child thinks. *They're only going to get dirty again later. She just wants to bug me. It's not fair!*

"It looks like it's time to mow the lawn," Dad says.

Why? I like long grass. It's natural. He just wants to bug me. It's not fair!

"Clean out your lockers!" the principal orders.

Why? Mold is great! If I want old lunches fossilizing in the bottom of my locker, what is that to him? He just wants to bug me! It's not fair!

Children inevitably grow up, but sometimes they don't grow out of certain patterns of thinking. When given a command later in life, they think it's issued just to bug them. They never see the reason behind the command.

This happens even with Christians. Take Paul's instruction to pray, for example. Some of us chafe under the command, seeing it as one more dull, burdensome responsibility. To be sure, we'd never call it that—we'll smilingly call it "our Christian privilege" and do our best to forget it. We'll get ourselves busy with loads of other things so we won't be bothered.

What a tragedy!

When Paul told the believers at Colosse that they should pray, he was telling them it was absolutely necessary to make sure they had the correct orientation. When you pray, you pray to God almighty, the Creator of the universe. You get yourself oriented to the center of all things.

If you are oriented toward your society, then your life will be governed by that orientation. If you think in terms of relationships, societal ills, and societal opportunities, you will major on your society.

You can be oriented toward yourself. You can be inward-looking, concerned primarily or even exclusively with your own well-being. If that's the case, it's hard for you to see further than the end of your nose.

Or you can be oriented toward heaven. You can have your mind and your heart set on Christ, who is seated at the Father's right hand. That's the Christian orientation as Paul sees it.

It's not that Paul is disinterested in society or uncaring about the individual. Clearly he is interested in both. But neither of these orientations should take precedence over that basic, fundamental orientation of the Christian, which is to set his or her mind and affections on things above, where Christ is seated at the right hand of God.

One of the best ways of demonstrating that orientation, quite frankly, will be to become a man or woman of prayer. "Keep looking up," Paul tells us.

Now, I'm the first to admit that my prayer life is not what it should be. I suspect I'm not alone. Many of us probably struggle in this area of prayer. And yet what Paul says here is very straightforward indeed. He insists that people who want to live rightly before the Lord must be men and women of prayer.

Why is it difficult to keep looking up?

Lord, please help me to be oriented more toward heaven.

Praying with One Eye Open

Devote yourselves to prayer, being watchful . . . Colossians 4:2

The most rewarding things in life usually take discipline. If you hope to lose weight, you discipline your eating habits. If you hope to lead your team in scoring, you discipline yourself with a training schedule. If you hope to play the piano in Carnegie Hall, you discipline your practice times.

Prayer is no different. It is a discipline. Unless you build some discipline into your life, either prayer will not get started or it won't keep going.

Many people find prayer boring, and because the last thing they want is to be bored, they decide they won't pray. They do this even though they know God told them to pray, even though they know what it does. It's boring, so they don't do it.

Part of the reason is that they haven't disciplined themselves to get information about which they can pray. If you want to know how to pray for someone, do a study of all the prayers of the Bible. Investigate biblical praying, and then work your way through each one of those prayers, inserting the name of the person you are concerned about. That will keep you going a bit.

Then make sure you have all the information you can get about the ministries of your own church. When you see a list of small group studies or care groups, copy it and pray for each of them. Get a list of the missionaries your church supports, and pray for each one. Get information from the missions office about their needs and concerns. Keep yourself informed from Scripture about the will of God and from people about their circumstances, and notice what Paul says: You've got to be alert. Keep your eyes wide open to what is going on in the world around you, and pray accordingly. Prayer is a discipline of information.

Prayer is also a discipline of inspiration. Prayer is only effective as we pray in the Spirit. That means a disciplined life, keeping in step with the Spirit. It means that we are laying aside old ways, putting to death old lifestyles, and concentrating on all the instructions we've gone through in Colossians. As we discipline our lives, we begin to discover the inspiration of the Spirit.

Finally, prayer is perspiration. Notice that Epaphras in 4:12 is described as "wrestling in prayer." The word is "agonizing" in prayer, the same word Paul used in 2:1 to describe his own efforts.

Have you ever agonized in prayer? I have. I've agonized to try to get some time to do it with everything else I have on my schedule. I've agonized to keep concentrating on it when I'm trying to do it. I find my timetable filled with good things, I find my mind filled with other things, and when I eventually find the time and the concentration, the phone rings.

You try and you try and you try, you look at the problems people have, and you say, "What possible answers are there to these things?" In prayer you take the burden off yourself and you roll it onto God. That's perspiration!

Where can you go to gather information that you can use to help you pray in a more focused way?

Father, please inspire me by your Spirit to know the things that are on your heart, the things you would like me to pray for.

Keep It Up!

Devote yourselves to prayer, being watchful . . . Colossians 4:2

It's not uncommon to see people start off in a big way and fizzle in a hurry. I much prefer to see people start the other way and grow.

In 1857, Jeremiah Lanphier invited the people of New York to meet with him to pray for a revival in Manhattan. Out of one million people, six came. But he stuck with it, and one year later six thousand people were meeting daily at the noon hour in the churches of Manhattan to pray for revival. Tens of thousands met in the evenings to pray for revival. The word spread to Chicago, and from Chicago to the mission fields of the world. This was known as the Third Great Awakening.

Have you ever thought of being a person who would keep his eyes on the throne, relate what he sees there to the people with whom he rubs shoulders, and pray that God would move among his friends, family, and acquaintances? Have you thought to make a declaration of your priorities in life by disciplining yourself to pray, despite all the other things that clamor for your attention? Might you be one who, through prayer, will keep looking up?

William Wilberforce, the author of *Real Christianity* and a personal friend of William Pitt the younger, could have been prime minister of Great Britain. He turned it down because he said he had two objectives: The abolition of slavery, and reformation of national morals.

"Boldly I must confess that I believe the national difficulties we face result from the decline of religion and morality among us," he said. "I must confess equally boldly that my own solid hopes for the well-being of my country depend not so much on her navies and armies, not on the wisdom of her rules, nor on the spirit of her people, as on the persuasion that she still contains many who love and obey the gospel of Christ. I believe that their prayers may yet prevail."

Would that apply to our nation at this time in history? What do we look to, our navies, armies, and air force? Our rulers? Are we looking to the president or to congress to pull us out of the mess? Do we look to the wonderful spirit of the people? Do we still quote that old Frenchman who came here a couple of hundred years ago who said that America is great because America is good? Are we pinning our hopes on these things?

Or do we believe that if anything is going to happen in America to turn things around and impact the world, that it will be God's people who know how to pray and who do it? I endorse what Wilberforce said. I believe this is a message for each of us.

Will you join me?

Do you know others who would be willing to join you in praying faithfully for our nation?

Father, I believe that if anything in our country is to change for the better, it will be because your people have been diligent and fervent in prayer. Please help me to be one of those people.

The Declaration of Dependence

Devote yourselves to prayer, being . . . thankful. Colossians 4:2

When invading Japanese armies forced General Douglas MacArthur to evacuate the Philippines at the outset of World War II, he made a famous declaration: "I shall return."

It wasn't a prayer, but at that stage of the conflict it might well have been. MacArthur was convinced the tide would turn, and he put himself on record as predicting it. He turned out to be right. He did return, and he vindicated his declaration.

Christian prayer is every bit the declaration that MacArthur's statement was. In fact, it's more so. When a person prays, he is making a statement. His prayer is first of all a declaration, not of independence, but of dependence. When a man or woman believes in prayer and practices it, that man or woman is declaring his utter dependence upon God.

Any Christian really thinking about it would have to admit that prayerlessness is sheer arrogance. If I don't bother to pray, what I am really saying is, "I can make it alone. I can handle this."

Often people who assume they can make it alone get into desperate straits. And then what do they do? They turn to God—and would you believe, they expect him to be waiting, listening, and ready with an answer yesterday. That's arrogance.

Conversely, the person of prayer is constantly affirming his or her dependence upon the Lord. Prayerfulness is evidence of faithfulness.

Prayer is also a declaration of delight. Notice that in verse 2 Paul includes the word *thankful*. When we pray, it is good to express our devotion. Whenever we sing praises in the community of believers, or hum while driving along the freeway, we express devotion to the majestic Lord.

Paul is especially interested here in the type of prayer we call "intercession," for he is asking that they pray on his behalf so that the ministry might go forward. But he also recognizes that thanksgiving and praise are an integral part of prayer.

When we turn to prayer and do it thankfully, we are expressing our gratitude to God. Common courtesy insists that we say "Thank you." If that's true in everyday, ordinary human activity, how much more so in reference to God? The believer is a person who, in prayer, is making a constant declaration of delight in God. He has a constant attitude of gratitude; he gives a continual paean of praise. That's what prayer means.

For those who know how to pray, prayer is a declaration of thankfulness and of sheer delight in who God is and what he has done.

How do you express your dependence on and your delight in God?

Father, thank you that I can call on you at any time, and you are available to help in both the most serious and the most everyday situations.

Pray for Open Doors

And pray for us, too, that God may open a door for our message, so that we may proclaim the mystery of Christ, for which I am in chains.
Colossians 4:3

Open doors are wonderful things. Without them, you could crash all day into the side of your refrigerator and never once get inside.

Open doors allow you to get to people. Closed doors keep you out. The apostle Paul apparently thought a lot about this.

More than once he talked about God opening doors of opportunity. After Paul and Barnabas had gone on their missionary journey, they returned to their sending church in Antioch and reported all that had happened. Among other things, they said that God had opened the door of faith to the Gentiles.

God has to open those doors if anything is to happen. Unless God intervenes, nothing of eternal consequence will be accomplished. As we become better equipped technologically, as we get our methodology oiled, honed, and improved, we sometimes think we can get the job done by ourselves. How foolish that is!

When you deal with souls, you are dabbling in eternal issues. Ministry is a battle. And because the opposition is formidable, we need resources greater than our own technology, methodology, enthusiasm, and money. We need God to open doors.

Currently there are more than thirty countries that restrict missionary activity. Those thirty-plus countries account for two-fifths of the world's population. Humanly speaking, two-fifths of the world is nearly out of reach. What shall we do? Do we shrug our shoulders, or do we pray that God might open doors?

Andrew Murray put it this way: "There is a world with its needs, entirely dependent upon and waiting to be helped by intercession. There is a God in heaven with his all-sufficient supply for all those needs, waiting to be asked. There is a church with its wondrous calling and its sure promises, waiting to be roused to a sense of its wondrous responsibility and power. There is a world with its perishing millions, with intercession its only hope."

There are more people alive on earth at the present time than ever before. Of the billions of people on the face of God's earth, more than half are unreached with the gospel of Christ. At least one billion are eminently reachable, but aren't being touched.

So what are we doing about it? Are we the kind of people who declare our utter devotion to the majesty of Christ through intercessory prayer? Or have we gotten so wrapped up in ourselves that we have lost sight of the God of the throne and of his world in intense need?

What are some "closed doors" that you can pray regularly for God to open?

Heavenly Father, please open the way for your people to share the gospel with those who have never heard.

Burn Out for God!

And pray for us, too, that God may open a door for our message, so that we may proclaim the mystery of Christ, for which I am in chains.
Colossians 4:3

Henry Martyn had a brilliant career as a mathematician at Cambridge University. While there he became involved in the church where Charles Simeon was minister. Soon he decided to go into the ministry and become Simeon's assistant.

After serving there a short time, he became the first volunteer to a new missionary society going out to India. The day he arrived at his new home he wrote in his journal, "Now let me burn out for God."

If Henry Martyn came back today, he'd look at all the books on burnout and say, "Great! All these people want to burn out for God!" But then he would read on and discover that they want to ensure that people *don't* burn out.

Now, I understand what these books are saying. I realize that people can get tired and exhausted. I understand and sympathize with it. But I also have a deep concern that many segments of the church lack any devotion to the ministry of Christ. People no longer say, "Let's do it, and if we burn out while doing it, hallelujah anyway!"

Henry Martyn translated the New Testament into Hindustani. When he finished that he translated it into Arabic. When he finished that, he translated it into Persian—and he was a mathematician, not a linguist. When he completed that, he died. He was thirty-one years old.

Paul was a man like that. He didn't sit in his prison cell saying, "Well, here I am stuck in prison. I guess I'll let those other guys do it now." No, he said, "Pray that God will open some doors—perhaps, first of all, that he'll open the cell doors here so I can get out. Next, pray for open doors that will allow us to get to places we haven't been."

Paul had the kingdom on his mind. He was committed to seeing his Lord's prayer fulfilled: "Our Father, who art in heaven, hallowed be thy name. Thy kingdom come, thy will be done on earth as it is in heaven."

Is that a prayer you've said recently? Have you asked yourself, "What exactly am I doing to bring about the establishment of the kingdom on earth so that the will of God might be done on earth as it is in heaven?"

What would you think of someone who found a cure for cancer but didn't share it? What would you think if he defended his silence by saying, "Well, it's very personal. I couldn't possibly tell you. Besides, I don't want to ram my cure down anyone's throat"?

You wouldn't be terribly impressed.

How often have you met people who profess to belong to Christ who say the same sorts of things about their faith?

We need to decide if what we have discovered in Christ is of greater significance than a cure for cancer. If it is, we had better determine to devote ourselves to him and to tell others what we know of him.

You can start by asking God to open a door of opportunity. Don't be surprised if he asks you to walk through it!

What are some of the ways you can work for God's will to be done in your home, in your church, in your community, and in the world?

Father, please help me to know how you would especially like me to work for your kingdom here on earth.

Work As a Team

And pray for us, too, that God may open a door for our message, so that we may proclaim the mystery of Christ, for which I am in chains.
Colossians 4:3

I got a letter one day from a Thomas Samuel, a missionary working among the unreached tribal villages of India. Christians had been praying that God would intervene in the utter pagan ignorance of these tribes. The area was suffering through a terrible drought, and believers began praying that God would send rain. He did.

The pagans who heard these prayers were convinced that God had heard and answered. They had lived through other droughts and knew the horrors they could bring. Now they began to turn to the Lord.

God was opening doors.

I received a letter from Argentina describing an evangelist who often holds a series of meetings in a great soccer stadium, where anywhere from fifty to eighty thousand people give their lives to Christ each week. That's fifty to eighty thousand Argentines per week who respond to the gospel. God is doing something utterly inexplicable in human terms.

God is opening doors.

Why does this happen? It happens because people take seriously the instruction of Scripture to pray that God will open doors. God works in response to the prevailing prayer of his people. He will change lives. He will change circumstances. He will intervene in government. He will intervene in nature.

God opens doors.

The encouraging thing is that he usually opens them wide enough so that several people together can get through. Evangelism is a team effort. Notice that Paul said: "And pray for us, too, that God may open a door."

Who is he referring to? The rest of the chapter lists all the people who worked with him, people with wonderful names like Tychicus and Aristarchus and Barnabas, Epaphras, Demas, Nympha, and Archippus. Paul called them fellow-soldiers, fellow-servants, fellow-sufferers. They were with Paul in ministry.

God usually does not work through a single individual. Normally he works through people who are knit together in a team. Nobody demonstrates that better than Paul.

It's obvious from his letters that people are with him, even as he is in prison. He is "in chains" as he writes this letter, but his friends are with him even there. They are part of the team. Paul says it is imperative that you pray for the team.

Why? For one simple yet profound reason. If the devil wants to stop evangelism, all he has to do is get Christians fighting with each other. It's so easy for him. If he wants to deflect people from what they're supposed to be doing, all he has to do is to get them squabbling. If he wants to make the work of Christ grind to a halt, he'll get people to major on minors.

When the apostle says, "Pray for us," he means it. He had a job to do, and he couldn't afford to get waylaid because people failed to pray for his team.

Who are the people on your team? Who do you pray and work with for the kingdom?

Dear Father, please knit your people together stronger and stronger as a team, and please help us to be unified in our desire to serve you.

On the Inside Looking Out

Pray that I may proclaim [the gospel] clearly, as I should. Be wise in the way you act toward outsiders; make the most of every opportunity.
Colossians 4:4-5

Who says God doesn't play football?

"God," Mike shouted, "if you'll let my kid score a touchdown, I'll be in church next Sunday!"

It was quite a statement. Mike hadn't gone to church in years, and he had no intention of going now. But desperation changes the rules. His son's football team had gone scoreless for six games, and he figured the only hope left was prayer.

On the very next play Mike's son was given the ball, a hole opened up in the line, and he raced sixty yards to score a touchdown. The crowd went wild, and Mike's buddies reminded him of his oath: "So, Saint Mike, you'll be in church next Sunday, right?"

"I'll be there," Mike promised. He had no trouble choosing a church, because sitting next to him was a Christian friend whose son also played on the team.

Mike came to church, heard the gospel, and came to Christ. Two weeks later his son became a Christian.

Why did it happen? According to Joe Aldrich, who tells this story, it happened because a Christian dad made a deliberate decision to make friends with non-Christians. When God intervened in Mike's life, a concerned Christian was there. Mike's conversion was no accident.

Paul's strategy was similar. The apostle not only asked that his Colossian friends pray that he and his companions might be effective in their ministry, but he reminds the

Colossians that they, too, have a ministry. While in verse 4 he says, "Pray that I may proclaim [the gospel] clearly, as I should," in verse 5 he immediately applies to it them and says, "Be wise in the way you act toward outsiders."

He reminds them that sharing the gospel is not the job of a favored elite or a small group of professionals. It is the work of all believers.

"I believed; therefore I have spoken," says the Old Testament as quoted by Paul in 2 Corinthians 4:13. "Let the redeemed of the LORD say this," says Psalm 107:2. And Romans 10:9 reminds us that if we confess with our mouth as well as believe in our heart, we will be saved. Open articulation of the faith is part and parcel of every Christian's spiritual experience.

Many people admit they feel desperately inadequate to the task. If you feel like this, join the club. Lots of us feel the same way. Don't worry about feeling inadequate; feel worried if you don't feel inadequate. Anybody who glibly and superficially storms into the business of communicating the Christian gospel has not understood the sheer immensity of what he is doing.

What activities are you involved in where you have opportunity to interact with non-Christians on a regular basis?

Dear Lord, please help me to be ready and to make the most of any opportunity to share my faith with someone who may not know you.

Salty Speech

Let your conversation be always full of grace, seasoned with salt, so that you may know how to answer everyone. Colossians 4:6

Many years ago Jill was working with a group of young people, trying to encourage them and train them to go out and share their faith. They were going to visit the coffee houses and dance halls, and she asked me to have a final word with them. I agreed.

I told these young people that they must not forget that as soon as they began to talk to people about Jesus Christ, they were dabbling with eternal souls. They would be messing with eternal issues, and they were going to engage the spiritual forces of darkness. Their faces dropped quite dramatically as I explained all this.

My wife had a little talk with me afterwards.

"I took about four weeks pumping up these kids, and it takes you about five minutes to stick a pin in them," she said.

"All I did was to remind them that if they go out seeking to minister to people on any other basis than in the anointing of the Holy Spirit, anticipating his intervention through the power of God, they are going to fail," I replied.

She agreed with my theology, but not with my methods.

For anyone to speak adequately the message of Christ; to know what to say, how to say it, and whom to say it to; to say it in a way that will be understandable and will elicit a favorable response, demands more intelligence than the sum of every congregation in the world. It requires that God, by his Spirit, speak his Word through people's lips, under the anointing of the Spirit and with his own brand of miracles. That is what Paul is saying here.

He put it in very practical terms. "Let your conversation be always full of grace." Don't expect people to listen if at other times your mouth is as dirty and filthy as the rest of them. Make sure that what you say is "seasoned with salt," that it is appetizing and interesting, has a tang to it, captures their imagination, and holds their attention. And ask God to show you "how to answer everyone."

That doesn't mean you must have all the answers. It does mean that you're ready to hear their questions and then respond as best you're able.

You say, "Stuart, this makes me feel so inadequate!"

I hope it does. If you feel adequate in your abilities, you'll go out bumping around in your own power and make an absolute mess of things. Make sure you are inadequate, then get on your knees and pray for yourself and for others. Say, "God, intervene in my life and in their lives so that we might become adequate witnesses of Jesus Christ."

But be prepared for surprises. You never know how he might answer!

How can you be sure that your conversation is interesting and "appetizing" to others, and that you know how to answer their questions about your faith?

Father, when I am with people who don't know you, please help me to be especially aware of my need for your help in sharing my hope with them, through my actions and my words.

Unsung Heroes

Epaphras, who is one of you and a servant of Christ Jesus, sends greetings. He is always wrestling in prayer for you, that you may stand firm in all the will of God, mature and fully assured. Colossians 4:12

Not all great heroes have famous names. Some do their mighty works quietly, out of the limelight. I read of one such man the other day.

He had only a sixth-grade education. He was a committed Christian, and one day told his church that he wanted to teach a Sunday school class. He was told that none were available, but that he could round up a few strays and begin one with them if he'd like.

Eventually he gathered a class of thirteen rowdy boys, nine from broken homes. He loved those kids. He took them hiking. He played marbles with them. He cared, and his kids knew it.

Today, eleven of those thirteen boys are in full-time vocational Christian work. Howard Hendricks was one of those boys. Hendricks tells this man's story in his book *Teaching to Change Lives.*

The Colossians had a man like that in their corner. Epaphras was a man of prayer, and his prayer for the people in Colosse was that those who had started well might stand firm. He prayed that those who had moved into newness of life might become fully assured of it. He thoroughly believed that prayer helps growing believers to mature.

Can you think of one person who began to show signs of spiritual life, but who never matured?

Can you think of people who began to learn the things of Christ, but then saw the ground taken out from under them and are no longer assured of the truth of the gospel? I can. And I'm sure you can, too.

Do we pray for these people? Do we recognize that the only way they will be turned to God is if God, by his power, reaches out to them from heaven and touches them in response to the believing prayer of God's people?

Prayer moves God to open doors, helps mold people together, and helps believers to grow.

Are you engaging in that kind of prayer? What a tremendous need there is for people who will take this seriously.

John Wesley said, "Give me one hundred preachers who fear nothing but sin and desire nothing but God, and I care not a straw whether they be clergy or laity. Such alone will shake the gates of hell and set up the kingdom of heaven on earth. God does nothing but in answer to prayer."

I listen to a man like John Wesley, because he was a man in touch with heaven. He was a man who could translate the power of heaven into the situation on earth.

Wesley was credited, along with his little group of preachers, with saving Britain from something as drastic, bloody, and horrible as the French Revolution. He was instrumental in establishing hundreds of churches and winning thousands of people to Christ at a time when Britain was in dire and desperate straits.

He was a man who knew God.

So when a man like John Wesley says a thing like that, the church in all generations should listen hard and ask itself, "Are we a praying church that is in touch with the sheer power of God?"

The sooner we answer that question positively, the closer we are to recruiting the kind of force that Wesley envisioned.

Who can you pray fervently and regularly for, to be assured and grow in their faith?

Father, please help me to see people the way you see them, and to pray for them in the way that you know they need to be prayed for.

Meditations on the Active Christian Life

1. Copy 1 Samuel 12:23-24 on an index card, and put it in a place where you will see it each morning and be reminded how to pray.

2. Who do you think of when you read Ecclesiastes 4:9-12? What is so important about having a friend like this?

3. How could you develop some relationships like those Paul talks about in 1 Thessalonians 3:6-10?

4. Read thoughtfully through 2 Corinthians 5:11-21. How does this passage apply to you in your life right now?

5. Write down the commands in Hebrews 13:1-3 and verse 18, and under each one write down a few ideas about how you might carry it out in the near future.

How Can I Stay on Track?

One of the most valuable things you can take on a trip south of the border is a bit of advice: Don't drink the water.

One of the best items to pack for a canoeing expedition down a dangerous river is a caution: Don't stand up in the canoe.

And one of the kindest presents you can give a young man searching for love is surely this: Don't marry any girl who smokes the wrong end of a lit cigar.

Warnings. They're indispensable to life. If heeded, they can save you untold heartache and misery.

That's why Paul's letter to the Colossians would be incomplete without some sober cautions against enemies who would try to lure believers away from Christ. Warnings are necessary and good. Sometimes they can save your life.

Paul warned the church in Colosse about people who would try to turn them away from the Christ they had learned about and loved.

He says, "I tell you all this so that no one may deceive you by fine-sounding arguments."

Not infrequently you'll find earnest people who have been seduced by philosophy, psychology, futurology, or astrology. They've been wholly caught up in them, and they fail to do one simple, basic thing: They fail to test all their learning against what they have been taught in Christ.

When you do that, you're a sitting duck for any arguments that come your way. Dick Lucas, writing in his commentary on Colossians, says, "Nothing is so dangerous as feeble reasoning allied with fast talking."

It's not hard these days to find a lot of feeble reasoning allied with a lot of fast talking. Christians who don't take the trouble to make sure they're rooted and grounded in Christ are asking to be swept away.

These deceivers will come. They'll promise you all sorts of things. They'll say you're missing out on the real thing. Turn away from them, Paul says. Christ is all you need!

That Man's a Hijacker!

See to it that no one takes you captive through hollow and deceptive philosophy, which depends on human tradition and the basic principles of this world rather than on Christ. Colossians 2:8

The passengers were flying along at thirty-five thousand feet, minding their own business, doing all the things that passengers do once they are well into their journey. Suddenly they were interrupted by the sound of the intercom being switched on.

"This is your captain speaking," a voice said. "I have some good news for you, and I have some bad news. First the bad news: I regret to inform you that we are lost. And now for the good news: We are making excellent time."

Paul says we've got to understand that having begun our spiritual odyssey, we need to beware of spiritual hijackers. The words translated "See to it" actually mean "Beware," or "Keep your wits about you." It's possible for us to be shanghaied by teachers of "hollow and deceptive philosophy." The word translated "take you captive" is used to describe someone who moves into a shaky situation, takes over a person's life, plunders his property, and steals away the people themselves. *Kidnap* would be the word today, or *hijack.*

With hijackers, you start off the way you want to go and finish up where you don't want to be. Somewhere along the way somebody diverts your life.

How can you be on the alert? One of the best ways is to learn to recognize the methods of these hijackers.

Some will take you captive through "deceptive philosophy." The Greek term used here simply means "the love of knowledge." Paul warns against those who love to teach all kinds of things for the sheer joy of teaching so that you would learn for the sheer joy of learning, without ever realizing that the content has zero spiritual or eternal value. It is "empty and deceptive."

These teachers also will come with traditions that are purely man-made, Paul says. The word for "tradition" means to hand down. Many traditions can be terrifically helpful. If someone has invented the wheel, have him hand down wheels to you, and use what he has discovered.

Tradition is not fundamentally wrong, but it can develop into something that is. It's wrong when it perpetuates a ritual devoid of reality. It's wrong when it invites us to go through the motions with an emptiness of spirit. That's the idea behind verse 8.

Paul says these teachers will push the basic principles of this world. When he mentions "this world," he's talking about a system that has no time for God.

When people try to hijack your faith, they will divert your attention from what is right and good and true. They will pervert the gospel by putting other things in its place. As a result, they subvert the authority of Christ.

Rather than base all spiritual reality and life itself on Christ, they will build all kinds of high-falutin', high-sounding, highly intriguing, wonderfully attractive structures which are at the core empty and destructive. Before you know it, Christ is no longer the believer's authority.

Sounds a bit grim, doesn't it?

The warning is no less needed today.

Has somebody hijacked your faith? Are you continuing as you began? Are you constantly aware of how easy it is to get off track, constantly alert to the spiritual dangers that come your way? Or have you become so casual and unthinking that you've gotten hijacked and have even fallen in love with the hijacker?

Don't laugh! That's the sort of thing that really happens when people are hijacked.

It needn't happen to you. When hijackers turn up, recognize them, resist them, and stand fast in the truth you have learned in Christ. It's the only safe thing to do.

Are the spiritual dangers you face daily usually in the area of knowledge for its own sake, traditions without meaning, or simply the world's way of leaving God out of the picture?

Dear heavenly Father, please help me to be on the alert for these spiritual hijackers, and to keep looking to you to keep me on a straight course.

That's a Straitjacket You're Trying On!

Do not let anyone judge you by what you eat or drink, or with regard to a religious festival, a New Moon celebration or a Sabbath day. These are a shadow of the things that were to come; the reality, however, is found in Christ. Colossians 2:16-17

Legalists will speak forcibly about what we must not do. That's what the legalists in Colosse were doing. They were telling the Colossians what they shouldn't eat and what they shouldn't drink. "You shall not eat this, this, and this," they said, "and you should not drink that, that, and that."

Some of us have been exposed to this kind of legalism. People have tried to lay on us rules of behavior that have nothing to do with Scripture. Clearly the Bible sometimes says, "Thou shalt not." Clearly the Bible often says, "Thou shalt." I'm not talking about that sort of thing; I'm talking about people saying, "You shall not eat this, you shall not drink this, you shall not go there, you shall not do that," even though the Bible says nothing about it.

Legalism also tells you what you must do. Apparently these teachers in the church at Colosse were insisting that people should observe religious festivals, New Moon celebrations, and the Sabbath day in a particular way. Notice that the religious festivals were annual, the New Moon celebrations were monthly, and the Sabbath was weekly. They were trying to get people into a rigid pattern of behavior on an annual, monthly, and weekly basis.

All of us are occasionally guilty of insisting that people do certain things, that they go certain places, that they perform certain rituals and adhere to certain practices. The Bible is silent about it, but we insist on these things.

Whenever we do that, we have lapsed into legalism.

People straining under legalism are in bondage. They become nervous and uptight, wondering if it's OK to do this and not that, if they should be here and not there, if they're correctly dotting their *i*'s and crossing their *t*'s.

Notice Paul's rebuttal of this approach. He says, "Don't let those kinds of people judge you."

Legalists tend not only to lay out for you a system of behavior explaining what to do and what not to do, but often they go a step further and say, "If you don't do it this way, you're not spiritual." They judge you on the basis of their own principles of operation. Paul says there are two reasons you should oppose them.

First, these people don't understand that the things they are particularly concerned about are merely a shadow of what was fulfilled in Christ. They are confusing shadow with substance.

Second, while these people not infrequently are deeply into ritual, they're not especially interested in the deep, spiritual reality of which the ritual speaks.

If ever you find yourself coming into bondage to the systems of a legalistic-minded brother or sister, you need to take action. Don't let them put you in a box because you don't dot their *i*'s and cross their *t*'s. Paul says it's more than likely they are confusing shadow with substance and substituting ritual for reality. You don't need that.

What you do need is a fresh appreciation for the grace and freedom that is in Christ Jesus, a grace and freedom that leads to true godliness as the Holy Spirit brings the truth of God's Word to bear on your life.

Rules can't make you holy. Legalism can't produce righteousness. All it's good for is producing a certain smugness that eventually ends in disaster.

What kinds of legalism do we tend to fall into today?

Dear Lord, please help me to stay close to you so I can know what you want me to do and not do—not so I can judge others, but so I can live in a way that pleases you.

That Balance Beam Is Tilted!

Grace be with you. Colossians 4:18

Many years ago Jill and I were talking with some English collegians who had returned home after their first year at university. We spent a whole wonderful afternoon answering their questions.

At the end of our time together, one of the students said, "Stuart, every single answer you have given has included 'balance.' A lot of it sounds like compromise to me. Can you explain the difference between balance and compromise?"

"That's the easiest question of the afternoon," I replied. "If you do it, it's compromise. If I do it, it's balance."

Balance. If there's one thing in the spiritual life we must maintain, it's balance. God's truth is often found in tension, and we must take care never to emphasize one aspect of truth over another. Let me give an example.

The Bible clearly teaches the sovereignty of God. It also clearly teaches the free will of man. That makes for some tension.

Some don't want to handle the tension, and so become either resolute free-will Arminians or staunch sovereignty-of-God Calvinists. The two groups separated centuries ago and have been shooting at each other ever since.

When people don't want to balance the tension, the easiest thing in the world is to opt for one side and take it to an unintended extreme—and create a breeding ground for heresy.

Paul always tried to caution against an extremism that disallows balancing aspects of truth. He taught the necessity of holding in tension the truths of Scripture so that no truth is pushed to a heretical end.

When he says legalism is out, he doesn't mean that anything goes. When he says asceticism is out, he doesn't mean we should become ill-disciplined slobs. We need balance. But balance, as important as it is, is not the key thought in Paul's message.

The central idea can be summed up in one word: *freedom*.

Paul writes to tell us that we are not to allow ourselves to be brought into bondage to anything, anywhere, anymore. He sums it up best in Galatians 5:1: "It is for freedom that Christ has set us free. Stand firm, then, and do not let yourselves be burdened again by a yoke of slavery." We are free!

"Free to be what?" you say.

"Free to be myself!" replies society.

"No, no!" says the Bible. "You're free to be Christ's. Therefore, don't let anyone bring you into any kind of bondage that would deny you the freedom to be exclusively his."

Let's get that clear! You are free to be Christ's, and to be his alone. This is true freedom—a freedom so invigorating, so full, lively, bracing, and dynamic, that it's impossible to fully describe. You have to experience it.

There's an enormous difference between talking about something wonderful and experiencing that wonderful thing for yourself. We could talk all day about the joys of being united to Christ or about the freedom you'll find in him, but until you make the trip yourself it will only be a report.

Don't settle for reports! Don't get waylaid by counterfeits! Experience Christ for yourself!

You were made for a glorious relationship with King Jesus, and only when you are rooted and growing and established in him will you truly enjoy all that life has to offer. When Paul ends his letters, "Grace be with you," that's what he's talking about.

Do you want fulfillment? Contentment? Spiritual health? Then stick with Jesus!

It's the only way to develop a spiritual stamina that lasts!

What does it mean to you to be "free to be Christ's alone"? What are you free from?

Dear heavenly Father, please release me from the specific things that tend to entangle me and prevent me from being free to be completely yours. Help me to experience the pure delight and freedom of life in Christ.

Meditations on Hanging in There

1. Notice, in Matthew 24:4-14, Jesus' warning to his disciples. What does this tell you about the importance of being wary of being deceived?

2. Acts 20:25-32 contrasts "shepherds" of God's "flock" with the "savage wolves." How can we tell the difference between the two, since both can come from within the church?

3. Galatians 1:6-9 uses very strong language to stress the importance of sticking to the one true, unchanging gospel. What does this imply about people who come in teaching something new and different?

4. What comes across as ultimately important in Philippians 3:1-11?

5. What principles given in 1 Timothy 4:1-5 help to identify false teachers?